-THE- Final Word

STANDING FIRM IN THE LAST DAYS

DONNA GAINES

MARGE LENOW

JEAN STOCKDALE

DAYNA STREET

ANGIE WILSON

The Final Word: Standing Firm in the Last Days

©2019 Bellevue Baptist Church

Cover and book design: Amanda Weaver

Contents

How to Use This Study

We are at war. Our enemy is real and is relentlessly engaged in schemes to neutralize us spiritually, rob us of joy, and take away our testimony. And with each passing day, the battle grows more intense. *The Final Word: Standing Firm in the Last Days* is a twelve-week study in spiritual warfare based upon Peter's teaching in 2 Peter and Paul's instruction in Ephesians 6 that will challenge believers to stand firm on the authority God has given to us through Christ.

This study is designed to provide an opportunity for personal study throughout the week leading up to a small group discussion and large group teaching time once a week. Each session is divided into five daily homework assignments that provide Bible study and personal application. The *Declarations of Who We Are in Christ* include a corresponding declaration of faith statement for each week's study.

In your small group time each week, you will be able to connect with other women and build life-giving, sharpening relationships. As you meet together, be ready to share what God has shown you through His Word using the weekly studies as a guide. In the large group teaching time, you will be challenged by relevant, biblical instruction that will encourage you to stand firm on the truth of God's Word. He has the Final Word!

2 Peter

Growth in Christian Virtue

1 Simon Peter, a bond-servant and apostle of Jesus Christ, to those who have received a faith of the same kind as ours, by the righteousness of our God and Savior, Jesus Christ: ² Grace and peace be multiplied to you in the knowledge of God and of Jesus our Lord; ³ seeing that His divine power has granted to us everything pertaining to life and godliness, through the true knowledge of Him who called us by His own glory and excellence. ⁴ For by these He has granted to us His precious and magnificent promises, so that by them you may become partakers of *the* divine nature, having escaped the corruption that is in the world by lust. ⁵ Now for this very reason also, applying all diligence, in your faith supply moral excellence, and in *your* moral excellence, knowledge, ⁶ and in *your* knowledge, self-control, and in *your* self-control, perseverance, and in *your* perseverance, godliness, ⁷ and in *your* godliness, brotherly kindness, and in *your* brotherly kindness, love. ⁸ For if these *qualities* are yours and are increasing, they render you neither useless nor unfruitful in the true knowledge of our Lord Jesus Christ. ⁹ For he who lacks these *qualities* is blind *or* short-sighted, having forgotten *his* purification from his former sins. ¹⁰ Therefore, brethren, be all the more diligent to make certain about His calling and choosing you; for as long as you practice these things, you will never stumble; ¹¹ for in this way the entrance into the eternal kingdom of our Lord and Savior Jesus Christ will be abundantly supplied to you.

¹² Therefore, I will always be ready to remind you of these things, even though you *already* know *them*, and have been established in the truth which is present with *you*. ¹³ I consider it right, as long as I am in this *earthly* dwelling, to stir you up by way of reminder, ¹⁴ knowing that the laying aside of my *earthly* dwelling is imminent, as also our Lord Jesus Christ has made clear to me. ¹⁵ And I will also be diligent that at any time after my departure you will be able to call these things to mind.

Eyewitnesses

¹⁶ For we did not follow cleverly devised tales when we made known to you the power and coming of our Lord Jesus Christ, but we were eyewitnesses of His majesty. ¹⁷ For when He received honor and glory from God the Father, such an utterance as this was made to Him by the Majestic Glory, "This is My beloved Son with whom I am well-pleased"— ¹⁸ and we ourselves heard this utterance made from heaven when we were with Him on the holy mountain.

¹⁹ *So* we have the prophetic word *made* more sure, to which you do well to pay attention as to a lamp shining in a dark place, until the day dawns and the morning star arises in your hearts. ²⁰ But know this first of all, that no prophecy of Scripture is *a matter* of one's own interpretation, ²¹ for no prophecy was ever made by an act of human will, but men moved by the Holy Spirit spoke from God.

The Rise of False Prophets

2 But false prophets also arose among the people, just as there will also be false teachers among you, who will secretly introduce destructive heresies, even denying the Master who bought them, bringing swift destruction upon themselves. ² Many will follow their sensuality, and because of them the way of the truth will be maligned; ³ and in *their* greed they will exploit you with false words; their judgment from long ago is not idle, and their destruction is not asleep.

⁴ For if God did not spare angels when they sinned, but cast them into hell and committed them to pits of darkness, reserved for judgment; ⁵ and did not spare the ancient world, but preserved Noah, a preacher of righteousness, with seven others, when He brought a flood upon the world of the ungodly; ⁶ and *if* He condemned the cities of Sodom and Gomorrah to destruction by reducing *them* to ashes, having made them an example to those who would live ungodly *lives* thereafter; ⁷ and *if* He rescued righteous Lot, oppressed by the sensual conduct of unprincipled men ⁸ (for by what he saw and heard *that* righteous man, while living among them, felt *his* righteous soul tormented day after day by *their* lawless deeds), ⁹ *then* the Lord knows how to rescue the godly from temptation, and to keep the unrighteous under punishment for the day of judgment, ¹⁰ and especially those who indulge the flesh in *its* corrupt desires and despise authority.

Daring, self-willed, they do not tremble when they revile angelic majesties, ¹¹ whereas angels who are greater in might and power do not bring a reviling judgment against them before the Lord. ¹² But these, like unreasoning animals, born as creatures of instinct to be captured and killed, reviling where they have no knowledge, will in the destruction of those creatures also be destroyed, ¹³ suffering wrong as the wages of doing wrong. They count it a pleasure to revel in the daytime. They are stains and blemishes, reveling in their deceptions, as they carouse with you, ¹⁴ having eyes full of adultery that never cease from sin, enticing unstable souls, having a heart trained in greed, accursed children; ¹⁵ forsaking the right way, they have gone astray, having followed the way of Balaam, the *son* of Beor, who loved the wages of unrighteousness; ¹⁶ but he received a rebuke for his own transgression, *for* a mute donkey, speaking with a voice of a man, restrained the madness of the prophet.

¹⁷ These are springs without water and mists driven by a storm, for whom the black darkness has been reserved. ¹⁸ For speaking out arrogant *words* of vanity they entice by fleshly desires, by sensuality, those who barely escape from the ones who live in error, ¹⁹ promising them freedom while they themselves are slaves of corruption; for by what a man is overcome, by this he is enslaved. ²⁰ For if, after they have escaped the defilements of the world by the knowledge of the Lord and Savior Jesus Christ, they are again entangled in them and are overcome, the last state has become worse for them than the first. ²¹ For it would be better for them not to have known the way of righteousness, than

having known it, to turn away from the holy commandment handed on to them. ²² It has happened to them according to the true proverb, "A dog returns to its own vomit," and, "A sow, after washing, *returns* to wallowing in the mire."

Purpose of This Letter

3 This is now, beloved, the second letter I am writing to you in which I am stirring up your sincere mind by way of reminder, ² that you should remember the words spoken beforehand by the holy prophets and the commandment of the Lord and Savior *spoken* by your apostles.

The Coming Day of the Lord

³ Know this first of all, that in the last days mockers will come with *their* mocking, following after their own lusts, ⁴ and saying, "Where is the promise of His coming? For *ever* since the fathers fell asleep, all continues just as it was from the beginning of creation." ⁵ For when they maintain this, it escapes their notice that by the word of God *the* heavens existed long ago and *the* earth was formed out of water and by water, ⁶ through which the world at that time was destroyed, being flooded with water. ⁷ But by His word the present heavens and earth are being reserved for fire, kept for the day of judgment and destruction of ungodly men.

⁸ But do not let this one *fact* escape your notice, beloved, that with the Lord one day is like a thousand years, and a thousand years like one day. ⁹ The Lord is not slow about His promise, as some count slowness, but is patient toward you, not wishing for any to perish but for all to come to repentance.

A New Heaven and Earth

¹⁰ But the day of the Lord will come like a thief, in which the heavens will pass away with a roar and the elements will be destroyed with intense heat, and the earth and its works will be burned up.

¹¹ Since all these things are to be destroyed in this way, what sort of people ought you to be in holy conduct and godliness, ¹² looking for and hastening the coming of the day of God, because of which the heavens will be destroyed by burning, and the elements will melt with intense heat! ¹³ But according to His promise we are looking for new heavens and a new earth, in which righteousness dwells.

¹⁴ Therefore, beloved, since you look for these things, be diligent to be found by Him in peace, spotless and blameless, ¹⁵ and regard the patience of our Lord *as* salvation; just as also our beloved brother Paul, according to the wisdom given him, wrote to you, ¹⁶ as also in all *his* letters, speaking in them of these things, in which are some things hard to understand, which the untaught and unstable distort, as *they do* also the rest of the Scriptures, to their own destruction. ¹⁷ You therefore,

beloved, knowing this beforehand, be on your guard so that you are not carried away by the error of unprincipled men and fall from your own steadfastness, [18] but grow in the grace and knowledge of our Lord and Savior Jesus Christ. To Him *be* the glory, both now and to the day of eternity. Amen.

Ephesians 6:10-20
The Armor of God

[10] Finally, be strong in the Lord and in the strength of His might. [11] Put on the full armor of God, so that you will be able to stand firm against the schemes of the devil. [12] For our struggle is not against flesh and blood, but against the rulers, against the powers, against the world forces of this darkness, against the spiritual *forces* of wickedness in the heavenly *places*. [13] Therefore, take up the full armor of God, so that you will be able to resist in the evil day, and having done everything, to stand firm. [14] Stand firm therefore, having girded your loins with truth, and having put on the breastplate of righteousness, [15] and having shod your feet with the preparation of the gospel of peace; [16] in addition to all, taking up the shield of faith with which you will be able to extinguish all the flaming arrows of the evil *one*. [17] And take the helmet of salvation, and the sword of the Spirit, which is the word of God.

[18] With all prayer and petition pray at all times in the Spirit, and with this in view, be on the alert with all perseverance and petition for all the saints, [19] and *pray* on my behalf, that utterance may be given to me in the opening of my mouth, to make known with boldness the mystery of the gospel, [20] for which I am an ambassador in chains; that in *proclaiming* it I may speak boldly, as I ought to speak.

Declarations of Who We Are in Christ

In Christ, I am a daughter of the King and my Father's name is Truth.
(Introduction)

In Christ, I am granted magnificent promises.
(Week 1)

In Christ, I possess the qualities I need for life and godliness.
(Week 2)

In Christ, I am created to bring honor and praise to The Majestic Glory.
(Week 3)

In Christ, I am protected and delivered by the Truth of God's Word.
(Week 4)

In Christ, I stand firm because He has the Final Word.
(Week 5)

In Christ, I put on the full armor of God to resist the attacks of the enemy.
(Week 6)

In Christ, I am set free. My chains are gone.
(Week 7)

In Christ, I have bold access to bring every prayer and petition to the throne of God.
(Week 8)

In Christ, I am on the alert and I overcome through persevering prayer.
(Week 9)

In Christ, I pursue holiness because I remember the promise of His coming.
(Week 10)

In Christ, I have victory and will reign eternally.
(Week 11)

To Him be the glory forever and ever—He is the Final Word!

INTRODUCTION

-THE-

Final Word

Standing Firm in the Last Days

Millions of spiritual creatures walk the earth unseen,
both when we sleep and when we awake.[1]
~ John Milton

Just because we can't see something doesn't mean that it is not there. In fact, only 4% of the universe is observable matter.[2] Just think about it. We can't see the air, but we know it exists because we live and breathe. We can see a brain, but no one has ever seen a mind, the place where our thoughts are born and live. Gravity. Radio waves. Atoms. Ultraviolet light. Infrared rays. No one questions the existence of these things unseen. Why? Because from our experience, we know that they exist.

Likewise, there is an ongoing cosmic conflict between the kingdom of light and the kingdom of darkness, between God and Satan, going on all around us. We cannot see it, but it is there. From our experience, we know it exists. The battle plays out on the world stage between nations, in families among different members, in churches through disunity that arises, and even within the divided heart of an individual person. We are in a spiritual battle. And although it is cosmic and vast, it is incredibly close and personal. Yet, often it remains unrecognized because much of the battle takes place in the invisible spiritual realm.

> *We are in a spiritual battle. And although it is cosmic and vast, it is incredibly close and personal.*

Paul explained this when he wrote to the Ephesians, "For we are not fighting against flesh-and-blood enemies [what we see with our physical eyes], but against evil rulers and authorities of the unseen world, against mighty powers in this dark world, and against evil spirits in the heavenly places [what we cannot see with our physical eyes] (Ephesians 6:12 NLT).

We see this reality fleshed out in 2 Kings 6. The wicked king of Aram is warring against Israel. Despite their best strategies, Aram cannot get the upper hand in the battle because God keeps revealing their plans to His prophet, Elisha. Convinced that a spy must be to blame, the king of

Aram calls his advisors in and asks them what is going on. They then explain that Elisha is foiling their battle plans with intel from the Eternal One. As a matter of fact, they tell him, the prophet even knows the words he says in his bedroom. Furious, the King of Aram commands his servants to go find Elisha and capture him.

The servants locate Elisha in Dothan, a city in the hills of northern Samaria. When they tell the king, he dispatches a great army of warriors, along with many horses and chariots, to capture one man, the prophet of God. During the night, the army encircles the city of Dothan. The next morning, when Elisha's servant awakens at dawn and goes outside, to his dismay, all he can see in absolutely every direction is the army of Aram. Panicked, the servant runs back inside and wakes up his sleeping master to ask what the plan is. Wiping the sleep out of his eyes, Elisha assures his frantic servant that God will have the final word, "Do not fear, for those who are with us are more than those who are with them" (2 Kings 6:16).

Chip Ingram writes:

> Elisha's servant must have thought that the old man had lost his mind.
>
> His prophecies may have been great, but his math was terrible. These two men were encircled by a vast army of professional killers, each zealous to satisfy the command of an evil king. The prophet and his servant were prepared for breakfast, not war. If ever a situation was hopeless, this was it. And Elisha calmly assured the man that the two of them had the upper hand.
>
> As the story unfolds, we see what Elisha meant. He prayed that his servant's eyes would be opened to the reality of God's army. When the attendant's eyes saw the usually unseen world, he was amazed. Behind Aram's bloodthirsty army on the hills surrounding Dothan were horses and chariots of fire—God's heavenly forces ready to fight supernaturally for the servants of God. For a moment, the invisible became visible, and it was incredible.
>
> For the enemy, the reverse was true; the visible suddenly became invisible. Elisha prayed blindness upon them, and when God answered, the prophet led the hostile army straight to the king of Israel and his forces, where the invaders were immediately captured. The invisible world turned out to be just as real as the visible world—and more powerful.[3]

This is the battle that is constantly warring around us. And it will continue to rage until God chooses to have the last final word at the return of Christ.

We Aren't the Only Ones

Sometimes it just helps to be reminded that we aren't the only ones who face relentless warfare. In Peter's second letter, he addresses a battle weary, scattered bunch of believers throughout Asia Minor who find themselves in conflict with both the seen and the unseen. Peter's countdown clock in life is expiring. Writing from a Roman jail, he is keenly aware that it will not be long until he is face-to-face with his Savior. And in what is his last testament, his message proclaims that God's grace (the desire and the ability to passionately live the will of God) through Christ is the transforming power that emboldens believers to live righteously in spite of opposition.

The seen conflicts these believers faced were suffering, persecution, strife, dissension, and heretical infiltration in the church. Dealing with one of those was bad, but the combo package was overwhelming. Peter wanted to encourage his recipients to stand firm and to instruct them on how best to do that. And what did he tell them? In short, they needed to cling to the knowledge of God, recognize the enemy who was behind the scenes waging war against them, and then realize that the days were growing darker as Christ's return was getting closer.

Paul's message is similar when he writes to the church at Ephesus just a few years earlier from a Roman prison cell. As we will discover in this study, both of their letters are sources of instruction and encouragement as we wait for the return of the conquering King.

What We Need to Know

Around the sixth century BC, Sun Tzu wrote a Chinese military treatise, *The Art of War*, in which he provides this profound military advice:

> If you know the enemy and know yourself, you need not fear the result of a hundred battles. If you know yourself but not the enemy, for every victory gained you will also suffer a defeat. If you know neither the enemy nor yourself, you will succumb in every battle.[4]

We must know the enemy. In Revelation 9:11, John calls him "the angel of the abyss; his name in Hebrew is Abaddon, and in the Greek he has the name Apollyon." *Apollyon,* means "Destroyer." That pretty much sums up human history. He is out to destroy everything in his path. Because he does not have the power to create, he will do the exact opposite—destruct and destroy. As Peter warns in his first letter, "Be of sober spirit, be on the alert. Your adversary, the devil, prowls around like a roaring lion, seeking someone to devour" (1 Peter 5:8).

In His power, we stand. Because of Calvary, we stand firm. Against the enemy, we stand our ground.

We must know ourselves. As believers, Christ lives in us and we are in Him. The One who lives in us is "greater than the one who is in the world" (1 John 4:4). In His power, we stand. Because of Calvary, we stand firm. Against the enemy, we stand our ground. We don't have to fight; the victory has already been won. We just have to put on our armor and stand.

A missionary who had just returned to the jungles of New Guinea once sent this letter to Ray Stedman:

> Man, it's great to be in the thick of the fight, to draw the old devil's heaviest guns, to have him at you with depression and discouragement, slander, disease. He doesn't waste time on a lukewarm bunch. He hits good and hard when a fellow is hitting him. You can always measure the weight of your blow by the one you get back.
>
> When you're on your back with fever and at your last ounce of strength, when some of your converts backslide, when you learn that your most promising inquirers are only fooling, when your mail gets held up, and some don't bother to answer your letters, is that the time to put on mourning? No, sir. That's the time to pull out the stops and shout, Hallelujah!
>
> The old fellow's getting it in the neck and hitting back. Heaven is leaning over the battlements and watching: "Will he stick with it?" And as they see Who is with us, as they see around us the unlimited reserves, the boundless resources, as they see the impossibility of failure, how disgusted and sad they must be when we run away.
>
> Glory to God! We're not going to run away. We're going to stand.[5]

As the world grows increasingly dark, the light of Christ will shine brighter. And as it does, our overcoming victory is in our faith, which takes us back to where we began. There is a battle raging that we cannot see with our physical eyes. There is an enemy that we cannot physically fight. But, Hallelujah, there is a Warrior King, who we call *Abba* Father, warring on our behalf. Hear Him singing over you, dear weary one:

> The soul that on Jesus hath leaned for repose,
> I will not, I will not desert to his foes;
> That soul, though all hell should endeavor to shake,
> I'll never, no, never, no, never forsake![6]

In the name of the One who exploded forth victorious from the tomb, plant your feet. Stand firm. Our Father has the Final Word!

WEEK 1

Magnificent Promises

Who We Are In Christ

Progress in the Christian life is made possible and practical by two factors:
the power of God and the promises of God.[1]
~ D. H. Wheaton

Do you love a good story? I do. You can often find me with my head in a book or my eyes affixed to my iPad, totally oblivious to the world around me. Unlike my children, who chose the books for their book reports based on which ones had the fewest number of pages, from my perspective, the more pages the better. And a complicated plot is an absolute necessity. Why waste time on a storyline that you figured out in chapter two? Every good narrative has a protagonist (hero) and an antagonist (villain). Much of the action centers around the conflict that transpires between the two. Usually, the protagonist triumphs in the end. God's Story is no exception. The protagonist—the Lord Jesus Christ—is introduced in the very first chapter of Genesis, and the antagonist—Satan—appears shortly thereafter. Thus, begins the unfolding of God's Story with countless twists and turns. Turn to Revelation 20:10, and you will discover Who wins in the end, though I think you've probably already taken a sneak peek.

When we become a part of God's Story as a member of His forever family, we pop up on Satan's radar screen, and his arsenal is targeted in our direction. Much of his ammunition is aimed toward our minds. While he cannot snatch us out of the Father's hand, he attempts to antagonize us, steal away the reality of our identity in Christ, and to negate the peace we find in "His precious and magnificent promises" (2 Peter 1:4). We do not have to cower before this antagonist for "His divine power has granted to us everything pertaining to life and godliness" (2 Peter 1:3).

Peter understood the danger of this enemy. He had faced him before. As he composed his farewell letter to the believers, he included both an encouragement and a warning—no less pertinent to us today. The *New Bible Commentary* notes about 2 Peter: "These truths are just as important for the contemporary Christian, facing the pressures of a multi-faith society or the seductive teachings of the so-called New Age, as they were for those to whom Peter originally wrote."[2] Let's delve into the truths Peter shared. Remember, we are on the winning team.

As we begin our study, shall we start with the controversy surrounding the book of 2 Peter? I presume that we should just get that out of the way. Through the centuries, there has been debate among scholars that the letter was a pseudepigrapha, a writing issued under a deceased person's name with content reflecting the kind of things that he might have said. Some of the reasonings behind this claim include a difference in language and style, a similarity between the letter and the book of Jude, the possibility that the content reflects a later date after Peter had died, and the reluctance of the early church fathers to include it in the New Testament canon. Nevertheless, 2 Peter was incorporated into the canon, which certainly vouches for its authenticity in light of the exacting standards for inclusion in the Scriptures.

This week, we will look at the first four verses in 2 Peter 1 which include Peter's salutation to his readers and an exquisite reminder of both God's power and His promises. Additionally, we will include any pertinent issues that relate to our theme on spiritual warfare.

Read 2 Peter 1:1-4.

1. How does Peter identify himself in verse 1 and what significance do you attribute to each?

2. How does Peter refer to the recipients of the letter?

3. Through what did the recipients acquire their faith?

4. What significance can be attached to Peter referring to Jesus as God and Savior in verse 1?

Clearly Peter was referring to Jesus Christ as deity according to the grammar, which indicates a reference to one person. This Christological passage equates Jesus as coequal with God in nature, which was sanctioned by the early church. In contemporary culture, however, people go to great lengths to redefine Jesus as a good man, a great teacher, or even an imposter, but certainly not God. Dr. Ed Hindson comments:

> Despite the current attempts of the public media to "repackage" Jesus for the twenty-first century, serious questions remain regarding His identity. Is He merely a vague spiritual entity, as some suggest? Did He simply live and die as a moral man, as others claim? Or was He really the Son of God? [3]

5. Let's review the following scriptures to determine what Jesus said about himself.

John 4:25-26

John 6:40

John 8:58

John 10:30

John 14:9

Dr. Hindson expands on these comments by Jesus:

> Jesus claimed to have come from heaven, to be equal with God, to be the very incarnation of God, and to represent the power and authority of God. There can be no doubt that He believed He was God. And yet what a man *is* speaks louder than what he *does*. Look at the character of Jesus and you will see a man without sin, a man who is pure before all men.[4]

6. Record what these people said about Jesus in these verses.

Simon Peter – Matthew 16:16	
John the Baptist – John 1:29	
Samaritans – John 4:42	
Disciples – John 6:69	
The Roman Centurion – Matthew 27:54	

Dr. Hindson continues:

> The Bible "shouts" to us that Jesus is God. His life and character displayed His deity in person. Those who knew Him best were most willing to testify of His divine nature. And even His enemies were compelled to admit, "Surely he was the Son of God!" (Matthew 27:54) [5]

Indeed, Jesus is the Son of God.

Yesterday in our study, Peter addressed the recipients of his letter as people with the same kind of faith—a genuine, resilient faith in Jesus Christ whom he identified as God and Savior. Thus, Peter affirmed the divinity of Christ, an essential for salvation. In verse 2, he continues with his salutation to the believers by giving them a prayerful, but typical, Greek and Hebrew greeting with a wish for grace and peace in abundance. Yet, Peter adds a deeper dimension indicating where grace and peace are found.

Read 2 Peter 1:2.

1. Where does Peter state that grace and peace originate?

The Greek word *epignosis* is defined in the lexical aids in the *Hebrew-Greek Key Word Study Bible* as full, complete, advanced, or perfected knowledge.[6] Here we see it connected to spiritual benefits attained through the knowledge of God. Peter indicated that this knowledge is available to every believer with a sincere desire to know God. This concept was in direct contradiction with the Gnostic doctrines of false teachers of the day who were claiming a special knowledge that was imparted to just a special few.

2. What do you think full or complete knowledge is based on?

3. What does Jesus declare about Himself in John 14:6?

4. What recurring theme do you discover in the following verses? Check in the NLT, if possible.

John 3:3

John 5:24

John 8:58

Since Jesus identifies Himself as Truth and proclaims that He speaks the truth, He should be the center of our worldview.

Since Jesus identifies Himself as Truth and proclaims that He speaks the truth, He should be the center of our worldview. But there is another one vying for our allegiance, Satan, a formidable enemy who offers another view and seeks to deceive us (John 8:44).

Steve Wilkens explains: "Biblical truth requires an integrity that corresponds to an even higher standard. When Jesus identifies His message and person as truth, it reminds us that Scripture's use of truth is grounded in the divine, personal reality of God."[7]

There is a world out there clamoring to tell us that no such thing as absolute truth exists and that a Biblical worldview is narrow-minded, out of date, bigoted, and, quite frankly, un-American. Basically, your worldview is the prism through which you view the world based on your beliefs and values. It can be subjective based on your feelings, which may be a faulty measurement. Or, it could be founded on culture or ideology. For example, socialism, which has been in the forefront of the political discussion in recent months as we went through a national election, would necessitate a worldview tied to what is best for the government rather than the individual. Obviously, there are countless worldviews, but which one is the right one and upon what is it founded?

This quote from Ergun Caner is beneficial in making a determination:

> The classic schematic for a worldview is *truth*. Truth must be defined by clear parameters and discernable logic. In Greek philosophy, search for truth became the standard for developing a worldview. Such a worldview would not be subjected to the whims of feelings, nor the shifting sands of politics. Truth must be truth in all ages to all people.[8]

5. Has your worldview been distorted by feelings or ideology? If so, how, and how will you correct it?

Today as I was writing this lesson, two things happened—I accidently placed my hands on the wrong keys on my computer, and I experienced the warning signs of a migraine headache. I might even conclude that perhaps the two issues were somewhat related, but I digress. The end result of each was similar. Misplacing my hands on the keys resulted in a random jumble of letters that were indiscernible. When the visual aura, or the squiggles, entered my field of vision, I could no longer see clearly. The same thing happens when the enemy infiltrates our minds with his lies and his worldview. Jesus Christ is the truth and speaks the truth, and we must listen to Him.

In their book, *The Unshakable Truth*, Josh and Sean McDowell write:

> This kingdom worldview—the Way of Jesus—may be spiritual in nature, but it affects every area of life. Jesus' worldview unlocks a very specific way of life, a way of knowing what is really true, a picture of being what God meant us to be, and the power to live that out based on our relationship with God. When we see and live by God's spiritual worldview, it combats darkness, injustice, and evil within the world.[9]

6. Peter emphasizes in verse 2 the importance of the believer's knowledge of our Lord Jesus. From your knowledge of Scripture, make a list of key elements concerning His nature and what He has done for you.

As we conclude our study for today, meditate on one scholar's insights:

> Jesus' life is matchless in every way. From His complete divinity to His perfect humanity, from His miraculous virgin birth to His supernatural ascension into heaven, and from His flawless character to His unrivaled teaching, Jesus towers above all other religious leaders.

Why is Jesus the exclusive path to God? Because He alone lived a sinless life, died a vicarious death, and rose from the dead. Jesus is the exclusive path to God because no one has ever or will ever live a life like He lived. His life was the perfect sacrifice for imperfect people who never could sacrifice enough to save themselves.[10]

Sandwich criticism between two kindresses.

Just this week my sweet husband passed by the chair where I was reading, gave me a kiss on the forehead, and said, "You are beautiful." Immediately, something deep inside rose up to reject his compliment. From my perspective, it seemed that perhaps it might have been true decades ago when we were newly married, but so much has changed since then. I won't bore you with the details, but believe me, it is extensive.

1. Whose opinion of yourself do you value most?

2a. Are there some echoes reverberating in your mind of what others have said about you in the distant past or only recently? If so, what?

2b. How do you respond to the memories?

While we do value what others think and say about us, our ultimate goal should be to grasp and appropriate what God says about us. This is what God says: "Therefore if anyone is in Christ, he is a new creature; the old things passed away; behold new things have come" (2 Corinthians 5:17). Do you believe it? Or do you hear the echoes of the enemy contradicting what God has to say? What you believe inextricably determines how you live your life. Satan will dispute God's Word, but remember Jesus is Truth, and He tells the truth. From *The Unshakable Truth*, we find this nugget: "If what you think or feel about yourself does not line up with how the Bible describes you, you are making yourself the victim of a case of mistaken identity."[11]

Frequently, in my prayers for others, I pray that they will see themselves from God's perspective, recognizing not only who they are in Christ, but also how God views their choices to live godly lives or continue in their sin. Today, our study will encompass the truth of who we are in Christ. Let's view ourselves from God's perspective.

3. How has what God's Word says about you affected your personal spiritual perspective?

4. Are you ever tempted to believe Satan's lies about you?

The first two chapters of Ephesians provide an excellent outline of who we are in Christ. A significant portion of our study today will focus on these chapters. Please do not begrudge the time that it takes. It will bless your heart. The Lord has been so good to us.

5. Read Ephesians 1 and 2 and make a list of what you discover relating to your identity in Christ.

My Identity in Christ	Reference

There is a tendency in the heart of mankind to think that we must perform in order to be the recipients of this identity in Christ. Dear ones, this is our possession at the moment of our salvation. A grace gift from God. We can do nothing to achieve it. We do not deserve it. We might not act like it. Yet it is ours. I love this explanation from *The Unshakable Truth*:

> Studying the Bible, attending church, and sharing our faith do not cause God to regard us as more redeemed, justified, sanctified, or adopted more as his child. He *already* sees us in these ways because they define who we really are. So we don't *do* our way into becoming God's adopted children; we don't *do* things to cause his divine nature to dwell within us. We are not changed from the outside in; we are changed from the inside out. As we live in relationship with Christ, we start behaving according to our new nature and do those things that God's children do—act like Christ.[12]

This study is so rich in truth that it compels me to share a few more passages with you. We have merely scratched the surface of the riches we have in Jesus Christ.

6. Read these passages, and notate the truths found within them.

Reference	Truth
John 1:12	
John 15:15	
Romans 5:1	
Romans 8:17	
1 Corinthians 2:16	
Colossians 1:22	
Colossians 3:3	

7. Take a few moments now to pray the following verses from Ephesians 1:18-19a for yourself and for those whom you love:

> I pray that the eyes of your heart may be enlightened so that you will know what is the hope of His calling, what are the riches of the glory of His inheritance in the saints, and what is the surpassing greatness of His power toward us who believe.

Once we understand who we are in Christ, we can continue the process of sanctification to be more and more like Christ. It becomes a part of our DNA. We do not dwell on what others say nor do we give sway to the lies of the enemy. We are confident because we know the truth.

You are who God says you are—nothing more, nothing less.[13]

Since the Garden of Eden, Satan has been voicing his lies to all who would listen, causing mankind to question God's veracity. The NIV translates Jesus's reference to Satan in John 8:44, "When he lies, *he speaks his native language,* for he is a liar and the father of lies"[italics mine]. Our native language is what comes naturally to us. And certainly, Satan has an affinity for lying and tries to turn every Christian's heart away from God's truth.

Jennifer Kennedy Dean relates her struggle with wholeheartedly believing truth:

> How many times have you heard that you will find peace if only you can make yourself believe who you are in Christ? And, indeed, the Scripture references "in Christ" many times. Yet I could never make myself believe it, hard as I would try. Then one day I realized that is because it is keeping the emphasis on me. "I am righteous! I believe it. I am accepted. I believe it!" and that was true, except I didn't and couldn't get it to settle in. How could I quit trying to force the issue and lean in to the present Jesus?

> I had an epiphany. It's not about who I am in Christ. It's about who Christ is in me. That shifted the center of gravity and it all clicked. No more working hard to believe, just being present to the Presence.[14]

In the spiritual realm, a battle rages for the mind of believers. We can turn our hearts toward truth, but it will require the renewal of our minds. And that is our topic for today.

Read 2 Peter 1:3.

1. As believers, what gift was awarded to us?

2. What is the source of this gift?

Satan speaks empty promises and offers useless provisions. Jesus grants everything you need. Everything – Absolutely everything. Do you grasp it, my friend? It's everything you need for life and godliness. It's yours.

3. Do you ever live in contradiction to everything Christ has bestowed on you? Why?

4. What instructions does the believer encounter from Romans 12:2?

The crucial element in renewing the mind is learning how to recognize Satan's lies, which might come at you from various directions—culture, life experiences, what others have said, etc. Without a concrete knowledge of Scripture, we are powerless to identify the falsehoods. In *The Search for Significance*, this explanation is given:

> Some of the influences on our minds have been very positive; some have been harmful. For good or bad, our thoughts have been shaped by years of parental modeling, friendships, past experiences, choices we have made, our culture, the media, and many other factors. Our perceptions about God and about ourselves do not usually change by reading a verse or two of Scripture. Renewing our minds is a lifelong process. It is often painfully slow, but diligent study of God's Word, trust in the Holy Spirit's power to change us, and the encouragement of other believers can produce minds and lives that are healthy, honest, and fruitful for the kingdom of God.[15]

We have a formidable enemy. Charles Spurgeon discloses:

> Instrumental in the fall of humanity, Satan has acquired a very vast experience in opposing mankind. Having tempted the highest and the lowest, he knows exceedingly well what the strings of human action are and how to play upon them. He watches first of all our peculiar weaknesses. He looks us up and down and soon discovers our faults. . . When the arch-spy finds a weak place in the wall of our castle, he takes care to plant his battering ram and begin his siege.[16]

Satan's battle plan is to prevent our minds from being renewed. Our strategy should be to render his attacks ineffective. But, how do you identify thoughts contrary to the truth? Jim Logan in *Reclaiming Surrendered Ground* states: "The difference is that when these thoughts are from the enemy, they come with strong coercive force that is different than the gentle constraining of the Holy Spirit's direction."[17] Satan accuses of sins long forgiven; the Holy Spirit gently reproves us of unconfessed sin.

> *Satan's battle plan is to prevent our minds from being renewed. Our strategy should be to render his attacks ineffective.*

5. What effective battle tactic can you adopt according to 2 Corinthians 10:3-5? (We will look at this in more detail in week 7.)

Tomorrow we will continue with strategies for the battle for the mind. In anticipation, reflect on the next question and prayerfully ask the Lord to give you the insight to answer it.

6. What lie has Satan whispered into your ear, and what truth from God's Word refutes it?

Victory is ours for the taking. By His power, Jesus Christ has granted us everything thing we need for the conquest. Aren't you thankful you are His soldier? We know Who wins the final battle. Hallelujah!

In our study this week, we have contemplated both our enemy, Satan, and our Savior, the Lord Jesus Christ. One fills our minds with lies while the other speaks only truth. Hence, the battle rages for our mind. Today we will consider some action steps to victory over deception. Robert McGee in *The Search for Significance* relates:

> If false beliefs remain in our minds, unchallenged and unrejected, they retain an unconscious influence on our emotions and reactions. Consequently, our warfare is a sustained and continuous battle. Every disturbing situation provides us with an opportunity to discover our incorrect thinking, to reject our world-acquired beliefs, and exchange them for truth. This is a daily process for every Christian; only this aggressive, conscious, truth-seeking effort can reverse years of habitually wrong thinking.[18]

Every Christian struggles with faulty thinking patterns to some degree based on background and life experience (including culture, spiritual maturity, and knowledge of the Word). Victory will never be achieved through self-effort, but rather a reliance on the power of the Holy Spirit.

1. Record what Jesus relayed to His disciples concerning the ministry of the Holy Spirit in the believer's life in the following verses.

   John 14:16-17, 26

   John 16:13

The Spirit of Truth will assist us as we sort through our thoughts and arrive at truth. Hopefully, these action steps will help you or someone you are mentoring navigate the process.

Action Steps

- Confess any unconfessed sin. Remember that the Lord does not bring up any sin previously confessed—only Satan does that. Rather, God places them behind His back, throws them into the depths of the sea, removes them as far as the east is from the west—He remembers them no more. Don't worry about any unconfessed sins you can't remember. God will remind you of those. Present yourself as a clean vessel before the Lord, ready to seek His face.

- Ask the Lord to reveal any wrong thinking patterns—Satan's lies—you adhere to rather than trusting in His Word. Record any revelations in a journal. This will be a work in progress.

- Research using an exhaustive concordance and other Bible study tools to locate scriptures that specifically relate to each issue. Chronicle them in your journal. Review these verses regularly and choose some of them to commit to memory. Speak them aloud when false beliefs come your way. It will encourage you and rebuke the enemy.

- Read the Bible every day as a dedicated student. Do not approach it casually or in a disorganized manner, but rather as one seeking to know God more intimately. Allow truth to lodge deep within your heart. It will change your life.

The steps are simple, but the results can be priceless as God reveals things we often do not see on the surface. If you have been walking with the Lord for a long time, you might believe that you have long since prevailed in this battle. Won't you take a moment to entreat the Lord's wisdom on your behalf?

2. Let's practice the action steps. Below you will find two lies Satan uses frequently that believers often succumb to. Research or choose a specific verse from memory that refutes the false belief. Add a third lie from your life experience.

- You are no good, never have been, never will be.

- God will never use you, your sins are too great.

- (Add your own here.)

What you believe defines your actions. This chart found in *The Search for Significance* visually represents what transpires when we convert our false beliefs into God's truth. The end results are Godly actions rather than ungodly actions. And that, my friend, is genuine victory.

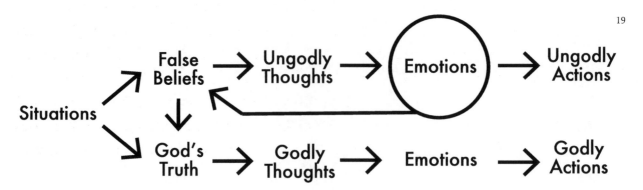

As we approach the end of our study this week, let's turn our attention back to our passage in 2 Peter. In his farewell letter to the believers, he has declared that they have everything they need for life and godliness. And next, Peter issues a sweet reminder.

3. Read 2 Peter 1:4. What, according to Peter, has the Lord Jesus granted the believer?

4. Write the promises that are bequeathed to Christians in the following verses.

I Peter 1:4-5	
Matthew 28:20	
Philippians 4:19	
John 14:1-3	
John 14:27	
2 Timothy 2:12	
Isaiah 40:29	

These verses contain only a few of the countless promises to us from our Lord Jesus. Yet, the enemy may whisper doubt into your ear. Can you trust Him to keep them?

Over thirty years ago, we faced a huge crisis, one that threatened the very well-being of our family. The situation was very public and devastating, and necessitated that my husband begin his law practice all over again. We wondered how we would ever make it financially. I began to realize that I viewed my husband as my security and provider. So, in the midst of this situation, concern and anxiety plagued me. I began reading the Psalms and recording all of God's promises in a notebook. When fear would overtake me, I would claim the promises from the Psalms. And God began to reveal Himself to me. I discovered that God was our provider and that He would take care of us just as He promised in His Word.

Space does not allow me to share all that the Lord did for us, but in a very brief time frame, we received $20,000 in client payments. Keep in mind that it was over thirty years ago—that was a considerable amount of money. So, God took care of the big things, but He also thought about the little things, as well. They arrived anonymously in the mailbox—gift certificates for manicures and clothing at a lovely women's boutique. I perceived this message from the Father, "I love you. You are mine." He is a promise keeper. If He says it, we can count on it.

5. Think about a time when God kept His promise to you. What truths did you learn as a result?

Peter encouraged his readers to stand on the promises. It's a good word for us, as well.

Standing on the promises that cannot fail,
When the howling storms of doubt and fear assail,
By the living Word of God I shall prevail,
Standing on the promises of God.[20]

WEEK 2

These Qualities are Yours:

What We Have in Christ

If I were your enemy, I'd seek to dim your passion, dull your interest in spiritual things, dampen your belief in God's ability and His personal concern for you, and convince you that the hope you've lost is never coming back— and was probably just a lie to begin with.[1]

~ Priscilla Shirer

As we saw last week, God "has granted to us everything pertaining to life and godliness, through the true knowledge of Him who called us by His own glory and excellence" (2 Peter 1:3). Therefore, we are duty bound to respond with maximum effort toward living for Christ and aggressively pursuing personal holiness and practical righteousness as a lifestyle. A perfect and complete gift of salvation has been provided by God through Christ. Romans 6:23 says, "The free gift of God is eternal life in Christ Jesus our Lord." The gift is free. However, this gracious gift carries a weight of responsibility for all who have received it!

My husband and I have been blessed to participate in a number of international mission trips, teaching pastors and church leaders about evangelism, discipleship, and church planting. As the deadline for a recent mission trip loomed large, I paused long enough in my frenzied preparations to make a list of things needing my attention before I boarded the plane to parts unknown. Now I realize list making is second nature for many of you, but let's face it. I am not a list maker. I have a sanguine personality and details bore me! I tend to live in the moment and figure out life as I go. I am not recommending this lifestyle; I am merely telling you how I do it. Personally, I admire highly organized people who operate on a schedule with tight controls and rigid routines, but I have come to grips with the fact I am not naturally wired that way. I have to work very hard to incorporate even a marginal amount of organization into my frantically chaotic, but extremely rewarding life.

A dear friend, who is acutely acquainted with my topsy-turvy ways and loves me anyway, inquired about my preparations for the upcoming trip. When I told her that I was working on my list she said, "A list. Has it come to that?" She is well aware of the desperate nature of things when I am reduced to making a list!

I love my life, but even I will admit that it is nearly always characterized by a whirlwind of activity. Life is lived at a frenetic pace at our house. Let me remind you we no longer have children living at home. Since the boys moved out, the noise level has diminished, but the pace has not. In some ways, it seems to have increased. My dear husband and I both tend to live without being very systematic or structured. Life at our house is crazy, but it is very satisfying for both of us.

While our style of living is generally unstructured, I have deliberately overcome this natural bent in regard to my Bible study. I am a very serious Bible student. I came to know the Lord Jesus Christ as my personal Lord and Savior at the age of twenty-four, having been un-churched up until that point in my life. How I wish I had heard and understood the gospel as a child! I believe my young adult years would have been very different, but I came to terms with the fact that I cannot change the past. I only have control over my present choices and my future plans.

As a new follower of Christ, I felt I was lagging way behind other Christians, having come to know the Lord as an adult rather than a child. I was lacking in biblical knowledge and the ability to accurately handle the Word of God. With a newfound faith and a growing sense of urgency to catch up with my peers, I set about to study the Word of God. The more I read the Scriptures, the more I fell in love with Jesus. As my love for the Lord grew, so did my love for His Word. This led to a self-propagating cycle of love and devotion that served to fuel my passion for the things of God.

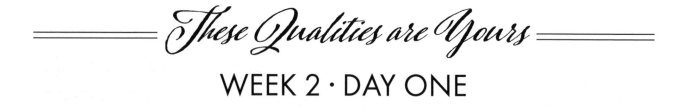

These Qualities are Yours
WEEK 2 · DAY ONE

Coming to know the Lord later in life was a point of shame and an embarrassment to me as a new Christian. You may have a similar experience. Or perhaps you received Christ as a child, but were not well taught in the things of God. Consequently, you failed Him miserably during your adolescent years. Now you have renewed your commitment to Him, but you are struggling with feelings of failure and shame. The great apostle Paul serves as a wonderful inspiration for me. He came to know the Lord late in his life, yet he did not let his past hold him back in the present from serving the Lord.

Read his testimony in 1 Timothy 1:12-16.

1. What was Paul's testimony?

2. What is your testimony?

While I believe a childhood conversion is preferable for many reasons, the amount of our sin does not damn us; the very fact of sin separates us from a holy God. Romans 3:23 says, "For all have sinned and fall short of the glory of God." We are all sinners in need of a Savior. However, one who receives Jesus in childhood will not have the same accumulation of the consequences of sin as the one who pursues "the passing pleasures of sin" (Hebrews 11:25) and then later comes to know Jesus as personal Lord and Savior.

> *The Christian life is to be a diligent pursuit of holy living.*

I would have rather come to Christ at an early age and have a testimony of a childhood conversion. Sadly, that is not my testimony. I wish I did not have the blight of sinful choices in my past, but I cannot change my personal history. I am grateful for my salvation and have learned to leave the incidentals of how and when it happened to the Lord. By faith I trust Jesus with my past, my present, and my future. I did not start strong, but I intend to finish well. Jesus is my Lord and heaven is my home! I do not have room in my life for lingering guilt over my past. I have determined to "lay aside every encumbrance and the sin which so easily entangles [me], and . . . run with endurance the race that is set before [me], fixing [my] eyes on Jesus, the author and perfecter of faith, who for the joy set before Him endured the cross, despising the shame, and has sat down at the right hand of the throne of God" (Hebrews 12:1-2). I trust you have made the same determination.

As a new believer I quickly learned the Christian life is not intended to be a passive experience. Christianity is not something that happens to you while you placidly live life. The Christian life is to be a diligent pursuit of holy living.

Read 2 Peter 1:5-15.

It is not enough to be born into God's family; we must also grow spiritually. This demands diligence and earnestness; a lazy, careless Christian does not grow. Peter then lists the spiritual characteristics that ought to be seen in the believer's life. He is not suggesting that we "add" these virtues the way we add beads to a string. Rather, each virtue helps us develop the next one. They are like the sections of a telescope: one leads into the other.

3. Look at 2 Peter 1:5-7. Make a list of the things Peter tells us to pursue and incorporate into our lives.

4. What do you need to work on in order to assimilate these traits into your daily life?

5. What plan of action will help you accomplish your assessment?

Lives characterized by godly character will prove to be useful and fruitful in the kingdom of God. If we fail to demonstrate these aspects of the Lord, we will likely be indistinguishable from the unbelieving world. Peter describes followers of Christ who are not bearing spiritual fruit as either "blind or shortsighted" (2 Peter 1:9). They have forgotten they "were like a firebrand snatched from the blaze" (Amos 4:11). They have failed to recall how God rescued them "out of a pit of destruction, out of the miry clay" (Psalm 40:2). How tragic!

Peter urges his readers to be "all the more diligent to make certain about His calling and choosing you; for as long as you practice these things, you will never stumble; for in this way the entrance into the eternal kingdom of our Lord and Savior Jesus Christ will be abundantly supplied to you" (2 Peter 1:10-11). Make certain you have met God on His terms of faith and repentance. Have the assurance of your salvation. Know that you have eternal life. This knowledge will (should) lead to progressive and personal righteousness demonstrated by the presence of godly characteristics.

When I was a child my mother used to say, "Practice makes perfect." This cliché was in reference to my foray into the world of musical instruments as I endeavored to master the piano. My dreams of becoming a world-renowned pianist proved to be short-lived. I quickly discovered I don't like to do anything I am not naturally gifted at because I simply loathe practicing! Oddly enough, the victorious Christian life takes practice. Who knew?

Read 2 Peter 1:1-15.

Peter is compelled to remind us of some things we already know. He writes, "I will always be ready to remind you of these things, even though you already know them" and to "stir you up by way of reminder." (2 Peter 1:12-13). Peter knows his death is imminent. He wants to be diligent to make sure his readers can quickly recall important spiritual truths after his departure. "Remember to remember," Peter is saying. If I could just remember all the things I have learned, I would be much wiser in the Scriptures and much farther along in my walk with God. The problem is, I quickly forget what I have learned! Can you relate?

Chuck Swindoll is one of my very favorite preachers, authors, and Bible scholars. He tells a story that is particularly pertinent to this passage. During his days as pastor of a church in Fullerton, California he usually drove in a separate car from his wife and four children. The demands of the ministry dictated that he be extremely flexible, especially after worship services. He said that he often drove home with one or two of the children in tow, while the others rode with his wife. One Sunday after church, the family came in the door and everyone scattered to change clothes while his wife made lunch. One by one, the family members returned to the kitchen to help get the meal on the table. As the pandemonium level rose and the endless chatter of a large family escalated, the phone rang. Chuck answered it and was startled to hear his youngest daughter say with great drama and exasperation in her voice, "Pastor Swindoll, do you know where your daughter is?" In the commotion, Chuck and his wife had forgotten their youngest daughter and left her stranded at the church! Isn't it amazing what we are able to forget?

Peter knows it is critical to our spiritual well-being that we become established in the truth and remember what we have already learned. Furthermore, if we fail to practice spiritual lessons we have learned, we will lose the spiritual truth we have gained more quickly than we learned it. In Luke 19:26 Jesus said, "I tell you that to everyone who has, more shall be given, but from the one who does not have, even what he does have shall be taken away." There is a biblical principle that cannot be circumvented. If we fail to practice and deliberately incorporate biblical principles into our spiritual lives, we will quickly forget these precious truths.

Learning spiritual truth is not like learning the multiplication table or a foreign language or the words to the national anthem. It involves much more than an exercise of the mind. Spiritual truth engages the entire being – body, soul, and spirit. Likewise, the child of God develops godly habit patterns and Christian character by practicing the disciplines of devotion. In Philippians 4:9 Paul writes, "The things you have learned and received and heard and seen in me, practice these things, and the God of peace will be with you." Practice makes perfect.

1. Look up Hebrews 5:11-14. How does the writer of Hebrews describe the immature believer?

2. How do we become successful in living the victorious Christian life?

When I first married, my husband drove a truck with a standard transmission. Try as I might, I could not master driving a stick shift. After getting the truck hung on an incline at a four-way stop sign and backing up traffic for what appeared to be miles, I resigned myself to defeat. How do you get good at driving a stick shift? How do you get to the place where you can seamlessly shift gears and drive smoothly? The answer is practice. Practice. Practice. Practice. The principle of practice we know to be true in the natural world also applies to the spiritual world. Otherwise, we are prone to forget what we know, rendering us "useless and unfruitful" for the kingdom of God.

That kind of spiritual forgetfulness leads to repeating old sins, and it robs Christians of their assurance. John MacArthur writes, "Assurance of salvation is directly related to present spiritual service and obedience, not merely to a past salvation event made dim in the disobedient believer's memory."[2]

Without question, sin continues to be an issue in the life of genuine believers. While we can never be sinless in this life, we will begin to **sin less and less** and hate its occurrence **more and more**. John wrote to believers, "If we confess our sins, He is faithful and righteous to forgive us our sins and to cleanse us from all unrighteousness" (1 John 1:9). We have "an Advocate with the Father, Jesus Christ the righteous" (1 John 2:1). Praise God, Jesus is our Advocate!

Believers often find themselves unable to confidently trust they have been rescued and redeemed from their former life when besetting sins erupt in their lives. Satan enters this scenario casting doubt on God and His Word, often resulting in the loss of the assurance of their salvation. If you do not have the assurance of your salvation, you will have great difficulty making progress in your faith walk, thus producing an anemic faith.

Beloved, if you are struggling with the issue of the assurance of salvation, may I share some insight with you? Gaining the assurance of your salvation is accomplished through an act of faith and is similar to your faith-based decision to receive the Lord Jesus Christ as your personal Lord and Savior. Trusting God to honor His Word concerning your eternal life is also an act of faith. This spiritual transaction is based on your total reliance on the truth of the Word of God and will be confirmed in your spirit by the Holy Spirit. John wrote:

> If we receive the testimony of men, the testimony of God is greater; for the testimony of God is this, that He has testified concerning His Son. The one who believes in the Son of God has the testimony in himself; the one who does not believe God has made Him a liar, because he has not believed in the testimony that God has given concerning His Son. And the testimony is this, that God has given us eternal life, and this life is in His Son. He who has the Son has the life; he who does not have the Son of God does not have the life (1 John 5:9-12).

By an act of the will, you take God at His Word and believe it. You relinquish your self-control and surrender your total being—body, soul, and spirit—to the Lord Jesus Christ and rest in His finished work.

3. Having the assurance of your salvation allows you the freedom to live in the sovereign grace of God. Read 1 John 5:13. What does this verse teach about eternal life?

What is the criteria for an ironclad assurance of your eternal security? In 2 Timothy 1:12, Paul writes, "I know whom I have believed and I am convinced that He is able to guard what I have entrusted to Him until that day." The same God Who can redeem you from the marketplace of sin is able to keep you eternally safe and secure.

4. Look up John 10:25-30. This is a precious passage on the eternal safekeeping of the child of God. What does Jesus say concerning the security of our salvation?

If you have met the Lord on His terms, repentance and faith, do not allow Satan to tempt you to doubt the assurance of your salvation. I urge you to go to the Lord in prayer and settle this issue "once and for all time." Confess any known sin. Tell Him that you will begin to walk by faith in this area. Thank Him for hearing your prayer and confirming your salvation. Write this date in the flyleaf of your Bible as the day you received the assurance of your salvation. Memorize Bible verses to battle Satan's lies with the truth of God's Word. Beloved, it is incumbent on us to become serious Bible students in order to know God's Word and to obey it through the power of the Holy Spirit. Beginning with the assurance of our salvation, we must believe God's Word, receive it by faith, and walk in obedience to it.

Peter gives us a list of important Christian virtues and admonishes us to diligently apply ourselves to their holy pursuit. The call to living righteously is therefore all the more needful as it renders us "neither useless nor unfruitful in the true knowledge of our Lord Jesus Christ" (2 Peter 1:8) and assures that we "will be able to call these things to mind" (2 Peter 1:15). This is how we stand firm in the last days!

Practice refers to the pattern of daily conduct. As we grow in the grace and knowledge of the Lord, we will increasingly pursue the moral virtues essential to holy living. This lifestyle gives silent testimony to a life consecrated to Christ. We will have no need to stumble into doubt, despair, or fear.

When we received Jesus by grace through faith, a spiritual transaction took place and "in this way the entrance into the eternal kingdom of our Lord and Savior Jesus Christ [was] abundantly supplied to you" (2 Peter 1:10-11). We were reconciled with a holy God and He became our Heavenly Father. We were placed in Christ. The Spirit of God sealed us for all eternity. Heaven became our final destination forever and ever. Therefore, we are compelled to practice holy living to know and enjoy the reality of our eternal salvation.

Satan's strategy is to dim our passion for the things of God, making us impotent and ineffective for the kingdom of God. Faith is fueled by passion for prayer, passion for God's Word, and passion for presenting an accurate depiction of His character as an image bearer of the Lord. No wonder Satan attacks us in this vulnerable area. If he can extinguish our fervor, he will have gained a toehold that he can exploit to build a stronghold of doubt and despair, often leading to depression. He will keep us from prayer by convincing us it is a pointless exercise. He will dampen our enthusiasm for personal Bible study and attempt to draw us away from the community of believers in our local church, leaving us feeling alone and abandoned. And he will damage our public testimony. This will serve to fuel our mounting guilt and heap condemnation on our despairing soul.

As we will see repeatedly throughout this study, Satan is a liar (John 8:44) and the way we fight his lies is with God's truth.

If you have fallen victim to Satan's ploys and find your passion for the things of the Lord to be waning, perhaps these verses can be your front line of defense. Personalize them and turn them into prayers, asking God to restore your passion for the things of the Lord.

"You will make known to me the path of life; in Your presence is fullness of joy; in Your right hand there are pleasures forever" (Psalm 16:11).

"The Lord is my strength and my shield; my heart trusts in Him, and I am helped; therefore my heart exults, and with my song I shall thank Him" (Psalm 28:7).

"You have turned for me my mourning into dancing; You have loosed my sackcloth and girded me with gladness, that my soul may sing praise to You and not be silent. O Lord my God, I will give thanks to You forever" (Psalm 30:11-12).

"Create in me a clean heart, O God, and renew a steadfast spirit within me" (Psalm 51:10).

"Restore to me the joy of Your salvation and sustain me with a willing spirit" (Psalm 51:12).

"Be devoted to one another in brotherly love; give preference to one another in honor; not lagging behind in diligence, fervent in spirit, serving the Lord; rejoicing in hope, persevering in tribulation, devoted to prayer, contributing to the needs of the saints, practicing hospitality" (Romans 12:10-13).

Ask God to help you be "zealous for what is good" (1 Peter 3:13). Beloved, this is how you will stand firm in the last days!

Like it or not, we are engaged in spiritual warfare. Too many Christians think we have boarded a cruise ship rather a battleship. Beloved, we are at war! According to Paul, our struggle is "against the rulers, against the powers, against the world forces of this darkness, against the spiritual forces of wickedness in the heavenly places" (Ephesians 6:12).

Beloved, we are battling Satan and his highly organized throngs of militant minions. To intentionally ignore or passively pretend it is not so is to surrender ground without a fight.

The Christian life is not a passive existence which results with our entrance into heaven through death or the rapture of the church. It is to be the active and aggressive pursuit of personal holiness and practical righteousness. As we see in 2 Peter 1:4, we are partakers of "His divine nature." Therefore, we are obligated to diligently grow in our faith.

Peter urges us to pursue spiritual disciplines such as diligence, moral excellence, knowledge, self-control, perseverance, godliness, brotherly kindness, and love. If we possess these virtues, we obviously belong to the Lord because these characteristics speak of Him. If they are evident and are increasing, we are "neither useless nor unfruitful in the true knowledge of our Lord Jesus Christ." Grow up. Suit up. Stand Firm.

1. Writing to Timothy, Paul uses three occupations to communicate spiritual truth. We will only look at the life of a soldier as it is most relevant to our study. Read 2 Timothy 2:3-4. What characteristics of a soldier's life should be evident in our Christian life?

2. Why?

3. What personal application can you make from this passage in regard to your Christian life?

Peter debunks the myth of a passive Christian experience. He recognizes we are locked in a spiritual battle with a fearsome foe. Thankfully, Jesus has defeated Satan. Through His death, burial, and resurrection, Jesus "disarmed the rulers and authorities, [and] He made a public display of them, having triumphed over them" (Colossians 2:15). Peter writes of Jesus' exaltation to the right hand of God "after angels and authorities and powers had been subjected to Him" (1 Peter 3:22). Ultimately, Satan will be "thrown into the lake of fire and brimstone, where the beast and the false prophet are also; and they will be tormented day and night forever and ever" (Revelation 20:10). Until then, we must be on guard. In these last days, the devil remains at large, "having great wrath, knowing that he has only a short time" (Revelation 12:12). Armor up.

Warren Wiersbe explains,

> God accomplishes His will on earth through *truth*; Satan accomplishes his purposes through *lies*. When the child of God believes God's truth, then the Spirit of God can work in power; for the Holy Spirit is "the Spirit of truth" (John 16:13). But when a person believes a lie, then Satan goes to work in that life; "for he is a liar, and the father of lies" (John 8:44). Faith in God's truth leads to victory; faith in Satan's lies leads to defeat.[3]

Satan cleverly disguises his lies with enough truth to make them plausible, especially to the believer who is poorly trained in "accurately handling the word of truth" (2 Timothy 2:15). Becoming well-grounded in the Word of God is imperative for the woman who is well aware of the spiritual battle raging around her.

As we saw in 2 Kings 6, spiritual warfare is the cosmic conflict waged in the invisible, spiritual realm, but simultaneously fleshed out in the visible, physical realm. To put it another way, the root of the war is something you cannot see, but the effects of the war are clearly seen and felt. This is because everything physical is either influenced or caused by something spiritual.

Behind every physical disturbance, setback, ailment, or issue we face lies a spiritual root. Unless we first identify and deal with the root's spiritual cause, our attempts to fix the physical problem will provide only temporary relief at best. In other words, everything that your five senses experience physically is first generated by something that your five senses cannot detect.

In light of this truth, you and I need to engage a sixth sense—a spiritual sense—when doing battle in this war. We must employ that which goes beyond physiology and address the spiritual root before we can truly fix the physical fruit. Here is the key to experiencing and living out on earth the victory that God has already secured in Heaven: to learn how to intentionally and effectively do battle in the spiritual realm.

Tony Evans explains,

> Satan often tries to prevent you from taking the spiritual realm seriously. If he can divert your attention away from the spiritual realm, he can keep you away from the only place where your victory is found. If he can distract you with people or things you can see, taste, touch, hear, or smell, he can keep you from living a life of victory. [4]

Satan attempts to cause us to doubt God, but that is not the only weapon in his unholy arsenal. He also desires to deceive us. In Revelation 12:9, John refers to him as he "who is called the devil and Satan, who deceives the whole world." However, God has not left us without adequate protection against the devil's deceptions. He has given us His indwelling Holy Spirit as our internal control and His Word as our external control. Battling Satan and his forces of evil will require both. The Spirit of God enables us. The Word of God instructs us. Faith must be activated. Dependence on the Holy Spirit is mandatory. Obedience to the Word of God is necessary.

Dependence on the Holy Spirit is mandatory. Obedience to the Word of God is necessary.

Through His Spirit and according to His Word, we can stand firm in these last days!

These Qualities are Yours

WEEK 2 · DAY FOUR

I feel compelled to issue a warning as we continue our study on spiritual warfare. There is a ditch on either side of the reality of this ongoing spiritual conflict. While Satan is a very real adversary, beware of assigning every interruption and annoyance in your day to the enemy of your soul. A flat tire, a dead battery, a car that won't crank may have more to do with lack of vehicle maintenance than spiritual warfare. Beware of giving Satan too much credit when things go haywire. This mindset will cause you to become overly sensitive to the enemy's activity in your life, blaming him for every mishap. Instead, shift your focus to the Lord Jesus and away from our archenemy in order to regain your spiritual equilibrium. Conversely, beware of minimizing Satan's attacks. We must stay on the alert. Satan will tempt you to doubt God as he did with Eve in the Garden. He will attempt to disrupt your prayer life and distract your devotional life in order to derail you spiritually. Satan's end game is to destroy your Christian testimony. Beware. Be warned. Be ready.

We are in Christ and His is our victory over Satan, sin, and self. Paul writes, "You have died and your life is hidden with Christ in God" (Colossians 3:3). Paul's prayer for us is "that the eyes of your heart may be enlightened, so that you will know what is the hope of His calling, what are the riches of the glory of His inheritance in the saints, and what is the surpassing greatness of His power toward us who believe. These are in accordance with the working of the strength of His might which He brought about in Christ, when He raised Him from the dead" (Ephesians 1:18-20). The same power that rose Jesus from the dead lives in us through His indwelling Spirit. God grant us eyes to see, ears to hear, and hearts to receive and believe this glorious truth!

When it comes to spiritual warfare, we must be educated and engaged. Paul writes, "We are not ignorant of his schemes" (2 Corinthians 2:11), but we are not to be paralyzed by unbelief or dominated by fear. Satan is a defeated foe. Be encouraged, sweet sister in the faith. Christ is our Victor!

Warren Wiersbe writes, "Satan cannot touch the child of God without the heavenly Father's permission. This is a great encouragement to us, for we know that whatever suffering may come to our lives, God has ordained it and is in complete control. The one thing God will not control is *how we respond to this suffering*, and it is here that Satan can gain his purpose."[5]

In keeping with this thread of thought, look with me in the book of Ruth. This love story is a perfect Old Testament depiction of the story of redemption. Ruth, a Moabitess, a foreigner, an idol worshipper, represents every sinner. Like Ruth, we were "excluded from the commonwealth of Israel, and strangers to the covenants of promise, having no hope and without God in the world" (Ephesians 2:12). Boaz is an Old Testament picture of the Lord Jesus Christ.

The story opens with Elimelech and Naomi, a Jewish couple, taking their two sons to Moab during a time of famine in their homeland, Bethlehem. Elimelech dies and both sons take Moabite wives, Ruth and Orpah. In short order, both sons die. Naomi determines to return to Bethlehem. Oprah chooses to remain in Moab while Ruth intends to accompany her bereaved mother-in-law to her homeland. As Naomi urges Ruth to remain in her native county, Ruth declares her love for Naomi and her allegiance to the God of Israel. Ruth's saving declaration is recorded in Ruth 1:16, "Your people shall be my people, and your God, my God." The destitute widows return to Naomi's homeland, Bethlehem.

In consenting to return to Bethlehem with Naomi, Ruth agrees to help support the aging woman. The biblical data suggests that Ruth was still quite young and physically strong. So, she goes to work in the fields, gleaning what the harvesters left behind in order to provide enough grain to eke out an existence.

John MacArthur notes,

> Biblical law established this as a means by which even the most destitute in Israel could always earn a living. Leviticus 19:9-10; 23:22, and Deuteronomy 24:19-21 all required that when a field was harvested, whatever fell from the sheaves should be deliberately left behind. When fruit was picked from trees and vines, some of it was to be left unplucked. The remains of the harvest were then free to be gleaned by anyone willing to do the work. [6]

1. Read Ruth 2:2-17. Ruth "went and gleaned in the field after the reapers." When Boaz saw an unfamiliar young woman gleaning in his field, he asked his workers about Ruth. What was their response?

2. When Boaz met Ruth, he instructed her to glean only in his field. What instructions had he given to his workers in regard to Ruth?

3. Ruth was humbled by the kindness of Boaz and asked, "Why have I found favor in your sight?" What was his response?

4. What did Boaz say to her at mealtime?

5. Reread Ruth 2:15-16. What additional instructions did Boaz give his workers?

6. Ruth gleaned "about an ephah of barley" which roughly translates to 29 pounds of grain. A typical worker could hope to glean one to two pounds on any given day. Ruth took the grain and her leftover lunch to Naomi. What was Naomi's response?

Keeping in mind that Ruth pictures a believer and Boaz is an Old Testament picture of Jesus, let's make some application in regard to spiritual warfare. Ruth "happened to come to the portion of the field belonging to Boaz, who was of the family of Elimelech." God providentially directed Ruth to the field belonging to Boaz. Beloved, we can rest in the Lord's providential care for our needs. As we yield to Him, He will lead us "in the paths of righteousness" (Psalm 23:3). Psalm 37:23 says, "The steps of a man are established by the Lord, and He delights in his way."

John MacArthur writes, "Nothing happens by "chance," but God is always behind the scenes, working all things together for the good of His people (Romans 8:28). There is no such thing as "luck" or "fate" for believers."[7]

Boaz comes to the field and takes notice of Ruth. We know the Lord sees us. He cherishes us. He values us. Jesus says, "Look at the birds of the air, that they do not sow, nor reap nor gather into barns, and yet your heavenly Father feeds them. Are you not more than they?" (Matthew 6:26).

In her book, *The Gospel of Ruth*, Carolyn James gives this insight,

> For me the moment that changes everything and that actually signals a turn for the better in Ruth's and Naomi's fortunes is when Boaz and his workers exchange greetings. What sounds at first like a simple "Hello!" and "Good morning!" – actually puts a stake in the ground to distinguish this barley field from any other place on the planet. Greetings couched in the richly intentional language of liturgy - "The Lord be with you!" answered by "The Lord bless you!" – should cause us (and almost certainly did cause Ruth) to sit up and take notice. Expectations soar, not in anticipation of a budding romance, but of something far more earthshaking, for the speakers are openly summoning Yahweh to be present among them. In a few brief words, we are suddenly presented with a hint that by wandering into this particular barley field the grieving, impoverished, socially isolated Ruth has discovered sanctuary. [8]

Boaz urges Ruth "not to go and glean in another field." He could provide for Ruth as long as she remained in his field. Jesus said, "Do not worry then, saying, 'What will we eat?' or 'What will we drink?' or 'What will we wear for clothing?' For the Gentiles eagerly seek all these things; for your heavenly Father knows that you need all these things. But seek first His kingdom and His righteousness, and all these things will be added to you" (Matthew 6:31-33).

Boaz encourages Ruth not to go glean in other fields but to "stay here with my maids." The female harvesters speak to us of the community of believers. If we are to be strong in the Spirit, we are not to be "forsaking our own assembling together, as is the habit of some, but encouraging one another; and all the more as [we] see the day drawing near" (Hebrews 10:25). We need to be intentionally engaged in a local church for instruction, encouragement, and fellowship. We were created for communion and community, first with the Father and then with His people.

Boaz "command[s] the servants not to touch" Ruth. Field hands were typically a rough bunch, and an unattached woman could be at risk for crude remarks, inappropriate touching, and even sexual assault. The Lord limits Satan's access to us as He did with Job with His hedge of protection (see Job 1:10).

We are under God's protection as long as we remain in His will, submitted to His authority. Nothing can touch our lives unless He ordains or allows it. Everything is filtered through the loving hand of God. What comes to us has been "Father-filtered."

Boaz invites her "to go to the water jars and drink from what the servants draw." This reminds us of Jesus' response to the Samaritan woman at the well. He said, "Whoever drinks of the water that I will give him shall never thirst; but the water that I will give him will become in him a well of water springing up to eternal life" (John 4:14). Revelation 22:17 says, "Let the one who is thirsty come; let the one who wishes take the water of life without cost."

Ruth questions Boaz's kindness saying, "Why have I found favor in your sight that you should take notice of me, since I am a foreigner?" Likewise, we were estranged from God, but Christ made a way for a sinner to be reconciled with a holy God.

Boaz pronounces a blessing on Ruth. "May the Lord reward your work, and your wages be full from the Lord, the God of Israel, under whose wings you have come to seek refuge." Ruth was under the protective cover of the God of Israel. In the same way, we securely dwell "in the shadow of the Almighty" (Psalm 91:1). Psalm 91:4 says, "He will cover you with His pinions, and under His wings you may seek refuge."

Boaz comforts her and speaks kindly to her. Jesus lavishes His unmerited favor on us. God "comforts us in all our affliction so that we will be able to comfort those who are in any affliction with the comfort with which we ourselves are comforted by God" (2 Corinthians 1:4).

Boaz invites her to dine with him and then serves her. That Boaz invites an impoverished foreigner to dine at his table and then serves her was counter-cultural. In Bible times, Israelites rarely mingled with Gentiles and men did not serve women, especially those of foreign descent. Psalm 23:5 says, "You prepare a table before me in the presence of my enemies." Song of Solomon 2:4 says, "He has brought me to his banquet hall, and his banner over me is love." In a post-resurrection encounter Jesus prepared a meal and invited His disciples to "Come and dine" (John 21:12 KJV). The invitation to come to His table is still open!

After the meal Ruth "[is] satisfied and [has] some left." This speaks of the overflow of God's blessings in our lives. Paul writes, "Now to Him who is able to do far more abundantly beyond all that we ask or think, according to the power that works within us, to Him be the glory in the church and in Christ Jesus to all generations forever and ever. Amen" (Ephesians 3:20-21).

Boaz tells his servants to "purposely pull out for her some grain from the bundles and leave it that she may glean." God is abundant in His grace and mercy towards those who believe. The psalmist wrote, "Blessed be the Lord, who daily loadeth us with benefits, even the God of our salvation. Selah" (Psalm 68:19 KJV).

Beloved, we have a very real enemy. We are engaged in spiritual warfare, but don't lose heart. Don't shrink back in fear. Don't waver in unbelief. We serve a God Who is greater than all. Psalm 27 is a favorite psalm of mine and my go-to passage when life gets either messy or miserable. "I would have despaired unless I had believed that I would see the goodness of the Lord in the land of the living. Wait for the Lord; be strong and let your heart take courage; yes, wait for the Lord" (Psalm 27:13-14). Beloved, don't despair. Let your heart take courage. Jesus has won the victory! That, beloved, is how we stand firm in the last days.

Promise Myself I will never say anything intentionally that I will regret.
Get thee behind me, Satan!

Tame my tongue.

Today we are looking at another Old Testament story as we continue our study in spiritual warfare, this one found in the book of Joshua. Joshua is an Old Testament book that depicts the New Testament victory we have in Jesus Christ. The man Joshua is a type, a picture of Jesus. Jericho was to be the first foray into battle for Moses' successor and the second generation of the Egyptian exiles who had been wandering in the wilderness. The Israelites had just entered the Promised Land, and this would be their first military campaign. Jericho was an impenetrable fortress protected by a formidable army. Taking the city surely seemed like a daunting, if not impossible, task for the children of Israel. The Lord spoke to Joshua, gave him a battle strategy, and God's people obeyed. The end result was victory. Hebrews 11:30 says, "By faith the walls of Jericho fell down after they had been encircled for seven days."

In the same fashion Satan has built strongholds in our lives as barriers to keep us from the fullness of Christ in our lives. How will these strongholds be pulled down and destroyed? By faith.

1. Read Joshua 5:13-15. Joshua was surveying the fortified city. Suddenly he was aware that "a man was standing opposite him with his sword drawn in his hand." Joshua asked, "Are you for us or for our adversaries?" What was the Man's response and what did Joshua do?

Joshua had a face-to-face encounter with the pre-incarnate Christ! Jesus made it clear that He had not come to take sides, but to take over! If we are to have any measure of victory against our adversary, we must have settled the Lordship issue. I am not talking about simply receiving Jesus as Lord and Savior at the moment of conversion. I am referring to the ongoing act of the will, giving Jesus His rightful place in our hearts! Jesus must be Lord of all. Peter addresses this issue in his first letter, "Sanctify Christ as Lord in your hearts" (1 Peter 3:15). Make Jesus Lord of your life. In season. Out of season. All the time. Sanctify Him in your heart. Give Him the rightful place as Lord of your life! There is to be a complete surrender to Christ as Lord that necessitates an ongoing yielding to His Lordship on a moment-by-moment basis. A divine paradox, but a necessary spiritual discipline that is required in order to abide in Jesus.

In His sermon, "The Triumph of Faith," Adrian Rogers said,

> God had given Joshua a promise. The Lord said to Joshua, "See, I have given Jericho into your hand, with its king and the valiant warriors" (Joshua 6:2). In the same manner God has given us the victory over sin, self, and Satan through Jesus Christ our Lord. Paul writes, "But thanks be to God, who gives us the victory through our Lord Jesus Christ" (1 Corinthians 15:57). Faith in God's promise was required in order to gain the victory over Jericho. We too must walk by faith, believing His promises revealed through His Word.[9]

2. Joshua took the Word of the Lord to the people. Read Joshua 6:3-5. What were God's instructions?

Joshua 6:8 says, "And it was so." The people obeyed! No dissention. No discussion. No suggestions of a better military strategy. The one Joshua presented must have seemed a bit sketchy, at least to those who had any experience in military strategy. But the people's confidence was not in the plan, but in the One who gave directions and promised victory. The people obeyed the Lord's Word given through His under shepherd, Joshua. Obedience. I want to press in on this spiritual truth. Obedience is required in order to be victorious in spiritual warfare. Obviously, obedience must be rooted in a working understanding of God's Word. You cannot obey what you do not know! In 1 Samuel 15:22, Samuel told King Saul, "Behold, to obey is better than sacrifice." Engaging in spiritual warfare against a well-trained, well-equipped, and ruthless enemy while unconfessed sin lingers in our lives will end in ignominious defeat. Obedience is required. A total dependence on the indwelling Holy Spirit is required. A settled confidence in Christ is required. Obedience. Dependence. Confidence. These are the essence of faith. "By faith the walls of Jericho fell down" (Hebrews 11:30).

3. As the Israelites marched around the city, what do you think the king and his mighty men of valor were thinking about God's people?

4. We can make a modern-day application. Look at 1 Corinthians 1:18; 1:26-28. What do unbelievers think about those who follow Christ?

Paul writes, "The foolishness of God is wiser than men, and the weakness of God is stronger than men" (1 Corinthians 1:25). When faced with a formidable stronghold we often resort to building our own strategy based on our reasoning. Instead, we need to seek the Lord and follow His direction. This action confounds unbelievers. When we obey His Word, depend on His Spirit, and trust confidently in the Lord Jesus, God is glorified. So, by faith march, children of God. March.

5. What do you think was happening in the hearts and minds of the Israelites as they marched around the massive walls of the great fortified city, armed only with trumpets?

Joshua instructed the priests to take seven trumpets and follow the ark of the covenant. The armed men were to march before the priests and the rear guard was to fall in behind the procession. If the people fixed their eyes on the walls of Jericho, surely fear gripped their hearts and caused their courage to melt away. But if the trumpet blasts stirred them to praise the Lord . . . And if the ark of the covenant, which represented the presence of God, became the object of their gaze . . . And if their army reminded them that God had promised them victory – then seven days of marching served to bolster their faith in a battle already won!

6. Back to our text. Read Joshua 6:15-20. What happened on the seventh day?

By faith the walls of Jericho fell. By faith the walls of Satan's strongholds will fall in our lives when we operate in the realm of faith. Faith consists of obedience to His Word, dependence on His Spirit, and confidence in Jesus to perform what He has promised. Warren Wiersbe writes, "Whenever God works in and through your life, it is always in response to faith. The thing that hinders the working of God is not his lack of power, but his people's lack of faith."[10]

As we saw last week, God, by "His divine power has granted to us everything pertaining to life and godliness, through the true knowledge of Him who called us by His own glory and excellence" (2 Peter 1:3). That promise includes what we need in order to emerge victorious in spiritual warfare. As Adrian Rogers said,

> There is no stronghold of Satan, there is no power of sin, that the child of God cannot overcome in the strength of the Holy Spirit. Isn't that wonderful? No power of Satan is so great that it can stand against you; there is no Jericho of sin that can withstand you, filled with the Holy Spirit. That's encouragement. There is no power so great you cannot overcome it. But you listen to me. There is no power of Satan so small that you can overcome it in the strength of your flesh.[11]

Satan hides behind walls of deceit. He loves darkness and shadows. He likes secrets. He has access to our minds and he plays and replays our past failures in a loop in our head. He uses shame and guilt to his advantage. Satan reaches into our past through our memories and into our future through imaginations. If our souls are not saturated with the Word of God and our wills predetermined to walk in obedience, we are easy prey for the prince of darkness and his minions. Thankfully, God has made a way of escape! By faith we capture every thought and speculation that is contrary to God and we ask Christ to crucify it.

When our oldest son had his driver's permit, we took every opportunity to have him drive in order to gain experience. Like most fifteen-year-olds, he was more than willing. One day on the way into school, we were on a winding street with narrow lanes and no shoulders. A street to his left intersected the road we were on and that street had a stop sign. Looking ahead I saw a driver approaching. Unfortunately, he disregarded the stop sign and pulled into the path of our car driven by our student driver. I placed my hand on my son's arm and in a calm reassuring voice I said,

"Get on your brake. Pump them gently and slow down." I didn't want him to overcompensate, jerk the wheel, and end up in the ditch. Our new driver scored high marks for handling the situation perfectly, avoiding hitting the careless driver, and keeping us safely on the road! Moral of this story? You cannot keep other drivers from disobeying traffic laws, but you can drive defensively and avoid a wreck.

Spiritual application? Satan has access to our minds. We cannot keep him from continually lobbing tempting thoughts in an effort to entice us to lie, or lust, or be jealous, or get angry, or criticize, or slander, or engage in gossip, or any number of ungodly allurements. But we do not have to allow his temptations to wreck us. We can tear down every barrier "erected against the truth of God, fitting every loose thought and emotion and impulse into the structure of life shaped by Christ" (2 Corinthians 10:5, MSG) and walk in victory. Beloved, this is how we will remain steadfast and stand firm in the last days.

Majestic Glory

The Attributes of God

God has no rival. He is subject to no other power and He reigns supreme. [1]

~ Charles R. Swindoll

Peter recalled the transfiguration of Jesus and the words of His Father by saying, "He received honor and glory from God the Father when the voice came to him from the Majestic Glory, saying, 'This is my Son, whom I love; with Him I am well pleased'" (2 Peter 1:17, NIV).

Majestic Glory! What a beautiful and accurate name for our God. We must strive to know more of His nature and character so that we are familiar with and dependent upon His attributes. This will empower us to stand firm in these last days.

Majestic Glory

WEEK 3 · DAY ONE

Before we spend the week looking closely at the attributes of God, let us consider His majesty and the truth of His Word.

David begins and ends Psalm 8 with these words, "O LORD, our Lord, how majestic is Your name in all the earth." Charles Swindoll notes, "The name of YHWH is identified with *majestic*, which derives from the Hebrew word *adar*, meaning 'wide, great, high, noble.' David pictures our Lord as One who is gloriously magnificent, absolutely majestic![2]

1. Take time to reflect on the majesty of God as you read these verses. Pray them back to Him as an offering of praise and worship.

   Psalm 19:1

Psalm 93:1

Psalm 95:3-6

Psalm 145:5

2. How do you see His majesty displayed day to day? (Consider creation, the human body, etc.)

In his second letter, Peter is warning Christians about the dangers of false teachers and emphasizing the importance of growing in their faith and knowledge of Jesus Christ. *The Life Application Study Bible* notes the following regarding 2 Peter 1:10-21.

> This section is a strong statement on the inspiration of Scripture. Peter affirms that the Old Testament prophets wrote God's messages. He puts himself and the other apostles in the same category because they also proclaim God's truth. The Bible is not a collection of fables or human ideas about God. It is God's very words given *through* people *to* people.[3]

In order to appropriate Scripture and use it to battle the enemy and his demons, we must wholeheartedly believe the Word of God. No exceptions.

3. Read 1 Peter 1:16-18. Why should we believe the words penned by Peter to be true?

4. What does 2 Timothy 3:16 tell us about the Word of God?

5. Has anyone ever challenged you on the validity of the Bible? Were you (are you) prepared to give a defense for what you believe?

6a. The tactics of the enemy have been the same since the beginning of time. Read Genesis 3:1. What did the serpent say to Eve?

6b. What does he imply about the character of God in his question?

7. Read Psalm 119:151. What does this verse tell us about God's Word?

If the devil can get us to doubt, even in the slightest way, the words we read from the Bible, he has us in his grip. We will more easily fall prey to his schemes and tactics. We will not be able to see God or hear from Him if we doubt Who He says He is. It is imperative that every follower of Christ emphatically believe the Holy Bible from cover to cover. God's Word is not a cafeteria line. We cannot pick and choose the parts we believe to be true and expect His favor and blessing to rest on us.

We will not be able to see God or hear from Him if we doubt Who He says He is.

His Word is not an allegory or a fictional story.

He IS majestic and His Word IS true!

This week, we will close each day reflecting on the ways God has revealed Himself to us. Use the letters below to list a characteristic of God. Look for a scripture that speaks to this attribute. Thank Him specifically for revealing Himself to you.

A

B

C

D

E

A right conception of God is basic not only to systematic theology but to practical Christian living as well. The man who comes to a right belief about God is relieved of ten thousand temporal problems. [4]
~ A.W. Tozer

What comes into our minds when we think about God is the most important thing about us.[5]
~ A.W. Tozer

Stop right where you are. Be still. Both in body and mind. Think of God. Consider Him. Who is He? What do you know to be true of Him?

We could never, in one week's study, cover all the attributes of Almighty God. However, I invite you to put all your heart and mind into focusing on and becoming convinced of Who He is!

We are in a battle, a spiritual war. As any good soldier would do, we must be armored up and prepared to face our enemy. Before we can wield our swords and shields, we must know our Commanding Officer and fully believe He is Who He says He is. What soldier would fight with all of his or her might for a cause they don't believe in? What army would run full speed ahead into a fiery battle on the word of a leader they doubt and question?

The same goes for every follower of Christ. We cannot and will not confidently confront our enemy, the devil, if we are not absolutely convinced that God is exactly who He says He is.

Today, we will look at God's attribute of **abundance**. It seems most fitting to begin here. If God lacks anything, how can we trust any other attribute? The devil, the father of lies and master deceiver, wants us to doubt God's omnipotence. If we undeniably accept the truth that His power is unlimited and He has the ability to do anything, we have a sure footing to learn and believe who He is.

1. Read John 10:10. Why did Jesus come?

2a. From a worldly point of view, what is abundant life?

2b. How does a Biblical point of view differ?

3. What do these verses teach you about God's character?

Ephesians 3:20-21

Luke 6:38

2 Corinthians 9:8

John 21:6

4. How have you experienced God as a God of abundance (overflowing, deep, weighty)?

Use the letters below to list a characteristic of God. Look for a scripture that speaks to this attribute. Thank Him specifically for revealing Himself to you.

F

G

H

I

J

How you view God determines how you approach Him or whether
you think He is approachable at all. [6]
~ Sylvia Gunter

In his book, *Victory in Spiritual Warfare*, Tony Evans writes, "One of the devil's main tricks is to cause you to miss the goodness of God."[7] If the devil can deceive us into doubting the goodness of God, we will not trust Him. We will hold back from wholehearted surrender if we question this attribute of our Father. Consider your earthly relationships. Would you confide in and rely on someone who did not have your best interests at heart? Of course not! The same applies to the relationship we have with our Heavenly Father. Doubting His goodness keeps us from a faith-filled life and from standing firm against the enemy of our soul.

Dinner was good. The movie was good. We had a good day. She is a good friend. We have all made similar statements as we evaluate various aspects of our lives. But as we do, we do so with an imperfect perspective in an imperfect world.

Today, we will ponder God's **goodness**. This attribute of the Father differs greatly from our human perspective of good.

1. What life circumstances have caused you to doubt or question the goodness of God?

2. Look up Psalm 119:68a. Write it out in the space below.

The Psalmist points us not only to God's character, but also to His actions. Naturally, He is good, and He also <u>does</u> good. Both His nature and His actions are good. Look at the second part of Psalm 119:68 and you will see the Psalmist asking God to "teach me Your decrees." I find it interesting that he makes this request after proclaiming the truth of God's goodness. How can we have an open, sensitive heart to the things of God if we do not fully believe in His goodness? It is vital that we trust

His nature and actions to be good before we are able to learn and, in turn, obey His Word.

3a. Read Exodus 33:18. What did Moses request of God?

3b. What was God's response in Exodus 33:19? What was He going to cause to pass in front of Moses?

Moses longed to see God's glory. And God's response to his plea was to cause all His goodness to pass in front of Moses. God's glory was God's goodness. This was true for Moses. And it is true for us.

4a. Read Psalm 84:11. What good things does God do for us according to verse 11a?

4b. What promise is contained in the second part of this verse?

Do you ever think God is withholding something good from you? Do you think Adam and Eve wrestled with a similar thought? Why would God give them access to every tree in the garden except one? Perhaps a better question would be why Adam and Eve insisted on having the fruit of the one restricted tree. Satan tempted Adam and Eve by drawing their attention to what they could not have. He tricked them into believing God was holding out on them, somehow keeping them from the one thing that would make them happy. In 2 Corinthians 12, Paul pleaded with God three times to remove a thorn in his flesh. God did not grant Paul's request. Rather, He responded with, "My grace is sufficient for you, for my power is made perfect in weakness" (2 Corinthians 12:9, NIV).

> *God's best thing is always better than my good thing.*

God's goodness is God Himself. His grace is all we need. His power is made perfect where we are weak. Perhaps our perception (Satan's deception) of His withholding a good thing from us is His good nature giving us His best thing.

God's best thing is always better than my good thing.

Use the letters below to list a characteristic of God. Look for a scripture that speaks to this attribute. Thank Him specifically for revealing Himself to you and for showing you His goodness.

K

L

M

N

O

Sylvia Gunter says that God's "role as Father is the most significant aspect of His nature."[8]

We will spend today looking at the **Father** heart of God. He is a gracious, loving parent who is "perfectly faithful, generous provider, loving and forgiving, a patient teacher, understanding counselor, wise and wonderfully communicating, strong yet intimate, affectionate and accepting and much more."[9]

Before we begin our study today, I realize many reading these words feel the sting of the absence of an earthly father. Perhaps you grew up without a father. Maybe your dad passed away when you were a child, or you missed his presence as a result of divorce. If you had an unreliable or absent father, for whatever reason, you may find it difficult to trust the Father heart of God. I encourage you to take a moment and ask the Lord, who loves and cares for you more than any human on the earth, to empty your heart of doubts about who He is in light of your earthly experiences. Ask Him to come in, by the power of His Holy Spirit, and blot out the wounds of your circumstances and to replace it with the truth of His character.

To be assured of and operate in the absolute certainty that your Heavenly Father will always be there is life-changing! Again, the devil wants you to doubt this truth. He will put forth his best effort to convince you otherwise.

Just as a parent is involved and interested in the details of their children's lives, God is involved and interested in the details of your life. Nothing gets by Him. Everything is important to Him. If it matters to you, it matters to Him. Why? Billy Graham offers a great answer.

> Why is God concerned not only about the big things but the small things in our lives? One reason is because He loves us. If He didn't love us, He wouldn't care what happens to us—and He certainly wouldn't care about the little details that often preoccupy us or cause us the greatest worry. But He does love us, and we know this because He sent His only Son into the world to purchase our salvation. Jesus said, "Even the very hairs of your head are all numbered. So don't be afraid" (Matthew 10:30-31).[10]

Knowing the Father heart of God is vital to stand firm against the tactics of the enemy. If Satan can cause us to feel abandoned, unloved, rejected, and alone, we will be less likely to go toe to toe with him in battle. He knows we will retreat and give him the upper hand without the confidence of the Father's love.

1. What do you see about the Father heart of God in these verses?

   Deuteronomy 32:9-11

   Isaiah 64:8

   Matthew 6:8, 26

   Zephaniah 3:17

2a. Review The Parable of the Prodigal Son in Luke 15:11-24. What characteristics of the father do you see that point to the heart of our Heavenly Father?

2b. How have you personally experienced this in your walk with God?

In *Prayer Portions*, Sylvia Gunter says, "Knowing Him as loving Father is the basis of enjoying intimate relationship with Him."[11] I'll take it a step further. Knowing Him as loving Father is the basis of standing firm against the schemes of the devil, fully confident that God has your back and will fight for you. Do not let the devil steal away the joy of knowing the Father heart of God.

If God is for us, who can be against us?
Romans 8:31b, NIV

Use the letters below to list a characteristic of God as your Father. Thank Him specifically for perfectly parenting you.

P

Q

R

S

T

As a child of God, the devil has no victory over you. He has already been defeated. When Jesus Christ died on the cross for you, breathed His last breath, and went into that grave as a dead man, the enemy erroneously declared victory. On the third day, Jesus did exactly what He said He would do. He came bursting forth from the dead and lives forevermore, seated at the right hand of the Father. He is interceding and preparing a place for you.

Al Mohler rightly declares, "For the Christian, the future is secured by the sure and certain fulfillment of God's promises and the comprehensive realization of Christ's reign over all powers in heaven and on the earth."[12] God is our **Victor**! This attribute of our Heavenly Father should give us courage and confidence to journey through this life, no matter what fiery darts the devil hurls at us. He is going down and he knows it. So should we.

Tony Evans says in his book, *Victory in Spiritual Warfare*, "Satan got pummeled at Calvary. Jesus Christ deactivated, dismantled and disarmed Satan's headship. Satan has lost his authority. Or, to make it more personal: Satan no longer has any authority over you."[13]

Tony Evans goes on to say,

> Satan and his minions have already lost this battle. Any advancement they make in your life or on this earth is because they have been given permission to do so. The only power they have is the power that is granted to them. Satan was able to get access to ruling planet earth only because Adam and Eve gave him permission to do it. Essentially, demons need permission from us to bring hell to us. Hell was told – either through sin or circumstance – that you were willing to yield.[14]

1a. If Satan has been defeated and has no authority over us, why do we sometimes experience oppression and feel the weightiness of his attacks?

1b. In what ways do we yield to the devil and his demons?

We are armed with the sword of the Spirit, which is the Word of God (Ephesians 6:17), as we come up against the evil one. Let's take time to look into the scriptures so we are prepared to wield our swords.

2. Read these verses and record your thoughts. Why/how can we live victoriously?

Deuteronomy 20:4

John 10:29

Hebrews 2:14-15

Billy Graham makes these observations about victorious Christian living.

> From the divine viewpoint, defeated Christians are abnormal. They are paralyzed members of the Body of Christ. Backsliding and carnality are not only inexcusable, they are incompatible with the normal Christian experience. They produce a regime of contradiction. Since the living Christ dwells within every one of us who has accepted Him as Savior, there is never any reason for defeat. No enemy is too powerful for Christ! These, then, are our three foes: the world, the flesh and the devil. The attitude of the Christian to all three of them is summed up in one word: *renounce*. There must be no bargaining, no compromise, no hesitation. Absolute renunciation is the only possible way for the Christian to have victory in life. If you are a Christian, there is no excuse for not having daily victory in your life by renouncing sin and, by faith, letting the Spirit of God have control of your life.[15]

3. Are there areas of life where you are experiencing defeat?

4. Where have you bargained, compromised, or hesitated? What do you need to renounce? (Consider sharing these with a trusted friend and asking her to pray specifically that you will allow the Spirit of God to have complete control in these areas.)

Use the letters below to list an attribute of God. Thank Him specifically for how He has revealed Himself to you in these ways.

U

V

W

X

Y

Z

At the mention of Your greatness, in Your Name I will bow down.
In Your presence fear is silent. For You wear the Victor's crown![16]
~ Darlene Zschech

The Truth Will be Maligned

Satan and His Fallen Angels

The existence of the devil is so clearly taught in the Bible
that to doubt it is to doubt the Bible itself.[1]
~ Chip Ingram

False teachers abound in our day. Just as in Peter's day, the enemy is behind the lies. Many of us would rather listen to someone who makes us feel better about our situation than to hear the truth. But the Bible is truth and presents us with life as God designed it to be lived. To deviate from His plan is to invite the activity of our enemy and ultimate destruction. We must choose to believe, and then God will begin to allow us to "see" all that He has revealed in His Word.

A popular blogger recently wrote a book that quickly went to the New York Times' Best Seller list. The book is listed in the category of Christian books. I was so proud of one of my daughters and her discernment after beginning to read the book and immediately recognizing the falsehoods. She later posted a warning on social media, to let other believers know the deception within.

False teachers quite often twist the truth or pervert it for their own benefit. So often, the lie is disguised in partial truths. Often, the distortion appeals to our flesh. That is why we must evaluate everything we hear and read through the grid of God's Word. To be able to recognize the deception, we must be well-acquainted with the Truth.

To be able to recognize the deception, we must be well-acquainted with the Truth.

In 2 Peter 2:1-9, Peter describes in detail what will happen to those who fall prey to the false teachers in the church, those who malign God's truth.

The Truth Will be Maligned

WEEK 4 · DAY ONE

1. Read 2 Peter 2:1-9. Who is behind the deception and falsehoods?

Satan is a real, formidable foe who cannot be taken lightly. Chip Ingram states:

> The two core Old Testament passages about Satan are Ezekiel 28 and Isaiah 14. Both of those passages point to dual realities, as much of Scripture does. Each speaks of a historical figure – the king of Tyre in Ezekiel and the king of Babylon in Isaiah – but those historical figures are windows into the true spiritual force behind them.[2]

2. Read the following two passages of Scripture and list what they reveal about Satan.

Isaiah 14:12-15

Ezekiel 28:12-17

C.S. Lewis gives insight into Satan's fall and the resulting impact:

> How did the dark power go wrong? Here, no doubt, we ask a question to which human beings cannot give an answer with any certainty. A reasonable (and traditional) guess, based on our own experiences of going wrong, can, however, be offered. The moment you have a self at all, there is a possibility of putting yourself first – wanting to be the centre – wanting to be God, in fact. That was the sin of Satan: and that was the sin he taught the human race."[3]

Read Revelation 12:3-9.

Revelation 12 depicts a great battle in Heaven. In this battle the enemy, Satan, is seeking to destroy the promised child, Jesus Christ. Verse 4 tells us angels were cast down with him. These angels are the demons who work to deceive and destroy mankind.

3. How many of the angels are fallen?

One of the devices Satan and his demons utilize to attack the church is deception and false doctrine. John MacArthur notes:

> There is nothing more offensive to God than the distortion of His Word (cf. Revelation 22:18-19). To falsify the facts about who God is and what He said—even promoting Satan's lies as if they were God's truth—is the basest form of hypocrisy. With eternity at stake, it is hard to believe that anyone would intentionally deceive other people, teaching them something that is spiritually catastrophic.[4]

Yet, that is exactly what false teachers do, with the intent of causing as much damage as possible. And not only are they deceptive, Peter tells us in 2 Peter 2:1 that these false teachers "secretly introduce destructive heresies."

4. What is heresy and how is heresy destructive?

The Greek word for heresies, *haireseis*, means "an opinion, especially a self-willed opinion, which is substituted for submission to the power of truth and leads to division and the formation of sects."[5] Peter is explaining that these false teachers have arrogantly exchanged God's truth for their own opinions, propagating destructive reasoning and lies.

In 2 Peter 2:2, Peter begins with the conjunction "even" to express how deep the false teachers' deceit has gone. The word "denying" means "'to refuse, 'to be unwilling,' or to firmly say no.'"[6]

5. How do false teachers deny the Master Who bought them and what is the result?

There is only one way we will be able to identify false teachers: we must be knowledgeable concerning the truth of the Word of God.

6. Read 1 John 2:26-27. What will keep us from falling prey to false teachers?

The deceit, the lie of the devil consists of this, that he wishes to make man believe that he can live without God's Word. Thus he dangles before man's fantasy a kingdom of faith, of power, and of peace, into which only he can enter who consents to the temptations; and conceals from men that he, as the devil, is the most unfortunate and unhappy of beings, since he is finally and eternally rejected by God.[7]
~ Dietrich Bonhoeffer

The Truth Will be Maligned

WEEK 4 · DAY TWO

When the Bible speaks of Satan, it is not speaking about an evil force, but a real created being. In his book, *The Invisible War,* Chip Ingram states,

> He is a powerful angel who committed treason against his Creator and convinced a third of the angels to rebel along with him. He now seeks to destroy all that is good and God-ordained, and his strategy ever since his fall has been to tempt us with the same agenda he had – to be like God. [8]

1. Read the following passages of Scripture and write the name or names revealed for Satan.

Scripture	Names for Satan
Genesis 3:1	
Matthew 4:3	
John 8:44	
John 10:10	
2 Corinthians 4:4	
2 Corinthians 11:13-15	
Ephesians 2:2	
Ephesians 6:11-12	
1 Thessalonians 2:18	
1 Peter 5:8	
1 John 3:8	
Revelation 12:7-9	

2. After reading these passages of Scripture, write out a description of the evil one and the ways he operates against mankind.

In 1527, Martin Luther, the catalyst for the 16th century Protestant Reformation, wrote "A Mighty Fortress is our God," a hymn based upon Psalm 46. As you conclude your time in the study of God's Word today, mediate on the truths of this great hymn of faith.

A mighty Fortress is our God,
A Bulwark never failing;
Our Helper He amid the flood
Of mortal ills prevailing:
For still our ancient foe
Doth seek to work us woe;
His craft and power are great,
And, armed with cruel hate,
On earth is not his equal.

Did we in our own strength confide,
Our striving would be losing;
Were not the right Man on our side,
The Man of God's own choosing:
Dost ask who that may be?
Christ Jesus, it is He;
Lord Sabaoth His Name,
From age to age the same,
And He must win the battle.

And though this world, with devils filled,

Should threaten to undo us,

We will not fear, for God hath willed

His truth to triumph through us:

The Prince of Darkness grim,

We tremble not for him;

His rage we can endure,

For lo! his doom is sure,

One little word shall fell him.

That word above all earthly powers,

No thanks to them, abideth;

The Spirit and the gifts are ours

Through Him who with us sideth:

Let goods and kindred go,

This mortal life also;

The body they may kill:

God's truth abideth still,

His Kingdom is forever.[9]

The Truth Will be Maligned

WEEK 4 · DAY THREE

We know that Jesus taught that the broad path had many traveling on it, but only a few would be on the narrow path that leads to life (Matthew 7:13-14). As we read 2 Peter 2:1-9, we see in verse 2, "that many will follow their sensuality." Christians are not those who go along with the majority. We are called to stand for Christ and sometimes that means we must stand alone. For those of us who are parents, it is important that we teach our children these truths.

God is righteous and just.

1. Read 2 Peter 2:2-9. What examples of judgment does Peter list?

As you read each of these examples, you see that God spares those who are righteous.

2. What determined their righteousness?

We are called to stand for Christ and sometimes that means we must stand alone.

Jesus, the Righteous One, is the only One to ever defeat the devil. He defeated him in life and death. It is only as we follow Christ and choose to die to our flesh that He might live through us, that we are victorious as well. Read the following quote from Ray Stedman:

> How does the devil plan to oppose the work of God in the world? By murdering, by destroying. One of the names given to the devil in the book of Revelation is *Apollyon*, which means 'destroyer'. What is it to destroy? It is to create chaos, to lay waste, to ruin, to make desolate. There you have the explanation for the whole tragic story of human history. A destroyer is at work among human beings.[10]

3. How do you see the destroyer at work in our day?

4. What are you doing to ensure that you and your family do not fall prey to the schemes of the evil one and his ultimate goal of destruction?

One of the greatest privileges we have as mothers and grandmothers is to pray for our children. For the next generation to withstand the enemy's attack upon them, we must intercede on their behalf. In her book, *Prayer Portions*, Sylvia Gunter has written the following Scripture-based prayers as a guide for us in this critical responsibility.

Prayer for Children

I pray that my children would:

Receive and love Jesus as their Savior – I pray that my children will understand that You loved them so much that You gave Your only Son for them, and that because they believe in Him, they will have life forever with You. John 3:16

Commit their lives to make Jesus Lord and be filled with Your Spirit – I pray that my children will recognize that Jesus is the Name above all names and will confess Him as Lord of all. I pray that they will trust Him with all their hearts, not lean on their own understanding, and acknowledge He is Lord in everything; thus, You will guide them in Your best way for them. May they be filled with Your Holy Spirit to the fullness of Christ. Philippians 2:9-11, Proverbs 3:5-6, Ephesians 5:18, 1:23, 4:13

Know the true and living God intimately and cherish and apply all Your names – I pray that my children will desire to truly know You, Father. May they love You, know You intimately, powerfully apply Your names, and rely on the character they represent in all their needs. Daniel 11:32b, Philippians 3:10, Psalm 9:10

Learn to pray and praise – I pray that my children will learn to communicate with You, their loving Father. Put Your praise in their hearts and on their lips continually. Lead them to be entirely dependent on You for everything, so they talk with You about all things and give You the honor and glory that You deserve. Mark 10:14-15, Matthew 21:16, Philippians 4:6

Know who they are in Christ – I pray that my children will know how precious they are to You. Teach them to base their identity and security on Christ. Give them Christ-centered confidence and Christ-centered worth. Give them Your mind about how You see them and how You feel about them. As Your creations, help them to fully know who they are and what they have in Christ and what they can do through Him. Ephesians 1:4, 7, 11-14, Colossians 1:27

Be protected from the evil one by the blood of Jesus – Protect my children by the covering blood of Jesus. I pray that my children will know the power of the blood to defeat all the works of the evil one. By the blood of Jesus, bind the enemy from interfering with Your perfect purposes in their lives. John 17:15, 1 John 4:4

Receive the love of God the Father – I pray that my children will know Your Father-heart and have the assurance of Your great love. Let them know by experience how extravagantly and unconditionally You love them. Father them with Your holy love, so that they know without doubt that You are always working in their lives in Your love. 1 John 3:1

Love the Word of God – I pray that my children will treasure Your Word more than wealth. Teach them to love Your Word and base their lives on it as their standard of life. Give them understanding as they humbly seek You in Your Word. Teach them to plead Your unbreakable promises and to defeat all the lies of the enemy with Your truth revealed in Your Word. Psalm 119:127-130, 159:1-62

Learn to hate sin and love holiness, righteousness, and the fear of the Lord – I pray that You will write Your word on the hearts of my children, so that they will choose the obedience of hating sin and loving Your holiness. Work in their lives the holy fear of You and the righteousness of Jesus. Help them not to just keep a set of rules, but to desire to please You in all they do. Create in them a pure heart. Make them wise in what is good and innocent in what is evil. Move in them to dedicate their lives to You as living sacrifices. Psalm 119:9,11; 2 Timothy 2:22, Romans 16:19b, Proverbs 8:13

Grow up into maturity in the Lord – I pray that my children will be built solidly on the foundation of Jesus and grow in Your grace with a conscious sense of Your presence conforming them to be like You. May they continue to be built up with Your wisdom, favor, truth, love, life, faith, strength, and thankfulness. Luke 2:52, Ephesians 4:15, Colossians 2:6-7

Glorify God in their bodies as Your temple – I pray that my children will honor You by keeping their bodies pure because they are the temple of Your Spirit. Teach them the great price You paid in the death of Jesus for their holiness. 1 Corinthians 6:19-20, Romans 12:1-2

Respect those in authority – I pray that my children will submit to the authorities You have placed over them as to You. Let them understand that You have established loving, wise covering for their good through parents and others in authority. Cause them to obey and not reserve for themselves the right to choose whether to obey, which You call rebellion. Give them a joyful, grateful heart as they submit to Your ordained authorities. Romans 13, Ephesians 6:1, 3:22-25

Have healthy, edifying, satisfying, wise friendships – I pray that my children will develop friendships based on the drawing of Your Holy Spirit to righteous companions. Give them friends who are true, wholesome, and mutually encouraging. Give them wisdom in choosing relationships that will honor You. Psalm 119:63, John 15:13-14

Know the truth and renew their minds in God's Word – I pray that my children will know Your truth in their hearts as well as their heads. May they base their life on Your truth instead of Satan's lies, so that they will experience all the freedom that Jesus died to give them. I pray that they will daily renew their minds in Your word and set their thoughts on what is true, noble, right, pure, lovely, admirable, excellent, and worthy of praise. John 8:32, Romans 12:2, Philippians 4:8

Walk wisely in the ways and wisdom of God – I pray that my children will be delighted with Your ways and Your wisdom, that they will commit everything they do to You and trust You to show them the blessings of obedience. Teach them to not trust in themselves, but to put You first in everything. Let their actions reflect the light of Your goodness, righteousness, truth, and wisdom in all they do. Day by day fulfill all Your will for them. Psalm 37:4-6, Proverbs 3:5-6, Ephesians 5:8-10, 15-17

Have the joy of the Lord – I pray that You alone will be the joy of my children. Fill them with Your joy inside, so they won't pursue the world's pleasures. Philippians 4:4, Nehemiah 8:10

Seek to please God, not self, and serve others – I pray that my children will desire to please You in their thoughts and actions and not be people pleasers. May they have servant's hearts and give to others like Jesus who did not seek to be served. Matthew 4:10b, Psalm 19:14, Mark 10:43-45

Learn who the enemy is and resist him victoriously – I pray that my children will humbly submit to God and resist the devil, thereby defeating him. May they discern the evil one's tactics and not entertain his lies in their thoughts nor be entrapped by his snares. I pray that they will receive Your strength and resurrection power for every spiritual battle. 2 Corinthians 2:11, James 4-7, Ephesians 6:10

Maintain their first-love devotion to Jesus – I pray that Jesus will be the first love of my children. Give them a passion for Jesus. Cause them to love Him with all their heart, soul, strength, and mind. I pray that they will prize His affection above all else. Philippians 3:13-14, Luke 10:27

Find the godly life partner that God is preparing, a mate who will complement them in their obedient walk with the Lord – I pray that in Your timing You will bring my children the life partners You have chosen for them. I trust that You are developing the character of Jesus in them. May their walk together with You be an undeniable testimony that You made them for each other. Make them a mighty witness for You. Bless them with Your best. Proverbs 12:4, 31:10; Psalm 112:1-2[11]

Jesus Christ came in the flesh to show us how to live. He was tempted in all ways just as we are and yet He never sinned (Hebrews 4:15). Christ was victorious that He might go to the cross, bearing our sin, and paying the penalty for it.

Jesus is our example. Just as He submitted to the will of the Father, we too must be fully surrendered to the will of our Heavenly Father. It is only in this state of submission that we find true freedom and victory over sin.

1. Read 2 Peter 2:9. How does the Lord rescue the godly from temptation?

2. Based on James 1:13-15, how does temptation turn into sin?

Jerry Bridges writes,

> In the deceitfulness of our hearts, we sometimes play with temptation by entertaining the thought that we can always confess and later ask forgiveness. Such thinking is exceedingly dangerous. God's judgment is without partiality. He never overlooks our sin. He never decides not to bother, since the sin is only a small one. No, God hates sin intensely whenever and wherever He finds it.[12]

3. How should we respond to temptation? Document your answer with Scripture.

The enemy schemes against us (Ephesians 6:10-12). We must recognize that our struggle is not against flesh and blood. Tony Evans, in his book, *Victory in Spiritual Warfare: Outfitting Yourself for the Battle* said, "The physical world simply manifests what is already happening in the spiritual realm. If you are unaware of the reality of the spiritual realm, you will be unaware of how that realm operates, causing you to be unprepared and ill equipped to live out your victory in your physical life." [13]

Think about a current struggle or concern in your life. Have you been battling in the spirit or giving in to worry, anxiety and scheming to solve the issue on your own?

4. How can you choose to do battle in the spirit realm and what scripture verses will you stand on?

Because we have a very real enemy, we must be on guard. Take a moment to slowly read 1 Peter 5:8, "Be of sober spirit, be on the alert. Your adversary, the devil, prowls around like a roaring lion, seeking someone to devour." Did you notice that he is seeking "someone"? Satan goes after the individual. He will come in through any door of sin that you open. Spend a few minutes asking the Holy Spirit to reveal any unconfessed sin in your life that the enemy could use against you.

The Truth Will be Maligned

WEEK 4 · DAY FIVE

Based on the Word of God, we know that our enemy is a defeated foe. Christ died for sin, ours personally and for the sins of the entire world (1 John 2:1-2). As we have already seen, because we are "in Christ" we have been given everything we need for life and godliness (2 Peter 1:3). Consequently, our response must be one of belief. We must believe God's Word and then appropriate it's truth in our lives.

I recently read Priscilla Shirer's book, *Fervent*. In this book about prayer, she recounted an incident when one of her sons was struggling with fear. He described a figure in detail that he said was in his room. It caused him to experience feelings of suffocating fear. This was all occurring at the time she was filming the movie *War Room*. She realized this was no coincidence and one day she declared war on the enemy. Priscilla said,

> That did it. I started to pray over him even more specifically, to pray over their room while the boys were away, to command this spirit of fear to leave my son alone in the name of Jesus. One day in particular when this issue seemed to be reaching a climax of intensity, I stormed into that bedroom like a rocket. I paced the floor, I quoted Scripture, I posted passages on the wall, I laid hands on the doorposts and window ledges.
>
> And I am not joking here, that was the last day my boy ever mentioned that man. As far as I know, he's never been bothered by it since to that degree or in that precise way…An enemy is after your children, I'm telling you. Believe it. Know it. But most important, deal with it – by tunneling deep into your prayer closet and fighting back with every parental and spiritual weapon at your disposal.[14]

1. Jesus defeated our enemy. Read Colossians 2:14-15 and describe how he has been defeated.

2. Read 1 Corinthians 15:55-57 and describe our victory.

3. Read 1 John 4:4 and relate how we defeat the enemy personally.

4. Read Revelation 20:7-10 and describe Satan's ultimate defeat.

5. Read Revelation 21:1-4 and recount our ultimate victory.

In opposition…to all the suggestions of the devil, the sole, simple, and sufficient answer is the Word of God. This puts to flight all the powers of darkness. The Christian finds this to be true in his individual experience. It dissipates his doubts; it drives away his fears; it delivers him from the power of Satan.[15]

~ Charles Hodge

Hillsong has written and recorded a song entitled, *Who You Say I Am.* The lyrics are beautiful. I would encourage you to listen to the song online. In the meantime, ponder the power of these truths put to music:

Who the Son sets free

Oh is free indeed

I'm a child of God

Yes I am

In my Father's house

There's a place for me

I'm a child of God

Yes I am

I am chosen

Not forsaken

I am who you say I am

You are for me

Not against me

I am who you say I am[16]

Hallelujah! The Lord our God, the Almighty reigns. He has defeated our foe. He is preparing a place for us. And as Jesus said, "If I go to prepare a place for you, I will come again and receive you to Myself, that where I am, there you may be also" (John 14:3). We must live with this glorious truth as our assurance. And in the eternal light of the Truth made flesh, may we live every day for "That Day"!

WEEK 5

The Flesh

Stand Firm Against the Schemes of the Devil

Were this an unfallen world the path of truth would be a smooth and easy one.
Had the nature of man not suffered a huge moral dislocation there would be no discord
between the way of God and the way of man. I assume that in heaven the angels live
through a thousand serene millenniums without feeling the slightest discord between their
desires and the will of God. But not so among men on earth. Here the natural man
receives not the things of the Spirit of God; the flesh lusts against the Spirit, and the
Spirit against the flesh, and these are contrary one to the other. In that contest
there can be only one outcome. We must surrender and God must have His way.
His glory and our eternal welfare require that it be so.[1]

~ A. W. Tozer

In his book, *The Divine Conspiracy*, Dallas Willard references a Gallup poll that indicates 94 percent of Americans claim to believe in God, 74 percent claim to have made a commitment to Jesus Christ, and about 34 percent profess to have had a "new birth" experience. He then notes, "These figures are shocking when thoughtfully compared to statistics on the same group for unethical behavior, crime, mental distress and disorder, family failures, addictions, financial misdealings and the like... Could such a combination of profession and failure really be the 'life and life abundantly' that Jesus said He came to give?"[2]

What possible reason can be given for such a discrepancy between a person's profession and practice? Perhaps those who made those statements do not really possess an understanding of commitment to Christ. However, most of us can probably list people who we think have made a genuine commitment to Christ, but whose lives are not on track with "the way of God" (see Tozer's quote). And if we were to be totally honest, we don't have to look much further than our own hearts to see this inconsistency.

The struggle between the flesh and the Spirit is real. As Paul wrote, "I do not understand what I do. For what I want to do I do not do, but what I hate I do...As it is, it is no longer I myself who do it, but it is sin living in me" (Romans 7:15,17).

The issue? Our flesh is rogue. It wants its own way and pursues its own ends. As a result, we often fail to practice what we profess to believe. As believers, we want to live a Godward life, but total submission to God does not come easily. Behaviors and attitudes from our old life hang around just waiting for a time and place to show out. And when we drop our guard, the enemy of our souls jumps at the opportunity to foster self-sufficient independence that is contrary to the will of God.

The plan of action? Learn to stand firm against Satan's scheming, destructive ways.

The Flesh
WEEK 5 · DAY ONE

Read 2 Peter 2:10-17.

The clock was counting down on Peter's remaining days on earth. As he continues to denounce the heresies and wrong motives of false teachers, Peter minces no words. He knows that his death is imminent and he wants believers to be aware of the deceptive ways of false teachers so that they will not fall prey to erroneous teaching, a trap set by the deceiver.

1. What descriptive words does Peter use to portray false teachers in verses 10-17?

2. Look back at the list of words you just compiled. Are there some present day false teachers who come to mind that fit that depiction today? (Please do not name them.) What words would you use to describe them?

Since the time of Satan's rebellion against God (detailed in Ezekiel 28), pride has been the principal characteristic of those who oppose God. As C.S. Lewis notes, "The essential vice, the utmost evil is

Pride…It was through Pride that the devil became the devil. Pride leads to every other vice. It is the complete anti-God state of mind."[3]

When Eve listened to the serpent, her independent decision to go after the forbidden placed her in direct opposition to God and in alignment with the enemy. Adopting a prideful, "anti-God state of mind," she established herself, the created, in an exalted place of superiority over the Creator. And there she stood. Right in the middle of Satan's destructive scheme.

In her book, *Fierce Women*, Kimberly Wagner points out, "Our pride treats God like He's not worthy of His position; He's not intelligent enough to run my life, and if His plan conflicts with mine—He needs to get out of my way."[4]

Does that sound painfully familiar?

3. Take a moment for self-reflection. Are there some areas in your life where pride rears its ugly head?

4. What are some verses that will help you overcome pride and enthrone God in His rightful position in your life?

The reason why many are still troubled, still seeking, still making little forward progress is because they haven't yet come to the end of themselves. We're still trying to give orders, and interfering with God's work within us.[5]
~ A.W. Tozer

Just like Satan, the words and actions of the false teachers Peter is denouncing were full of pride, arrogance, and presumption. They defied God by exalting their own fallacious teaching above His eternal truth. One erroneous teaching in particular that Peter calls them out on is that they doubted the existence of Satan and his demons. In verse 10, the phrase "angelic majesties" refers to fallen angels. John MacArthur explains Peter's terminology:

> The Bible indicates that even fallen angels retain the imprint of divine majesty, a shadow of their pre-Fall glory. In this sense, they are like sinful men—who still retain the divine image (Genesis 1:26; Psalm 8:5)—and post-Fall creation—which still evidences its God-given magnificence (1 Corinthians. 15:40-41). Thus there remains a transcendent amount of dignity for demons, even though they are fallen. The apostle Paul implied this when he referred to demons as principalities, powers, and rulers (cf. 2 Corinthians 10:3-5)—delineating at least three levels of majesty and authority within the demonic realm. Although they are certainly subservient to God, fallen angels (under the leadership of Satan) wield extensive influence and power in this world (John 12:31; cf. Ephesians 2:2). A powerful demon hindered the mighty angel Gabriel for twenty-one days from doing God's work until the archangel Michael and the most powerful angels came to help him (Daniel 10:13). Yet, the false teachers of Peter's day simply mocked demons fearlessly, presuming that they (as fallen men) were somehow greater than fallen angels.[6]

Similar to these false prophets, many in our current day deny the reality of the spiritual world and either deny or ignore the enemy's activity, a play right out of his evil playbook. Timothy Warner observes:

> Only eternity will reveal the number of believers who have led unproductive, frustrated lives and of Christian workers who have been forced to forsake their ministries because of attacks of the enemy. This happens in spite of the fact that the New Testament warnings concerning demonic activity are all addressed to believers...How RESIST got changed to IGNORE in so many segments of the Church, I don't know. When it did, however, Satan and his forces gained a great strategic advantage.[7]

The damage that has been done to the body of Christ just because so many refuse to recognize the influence of the enemy is devastating. Regardless of what the false teachers Peter was writing about thought, Satan has one plan and one plan only. Steal. Kill. Destroy. (John 10:10).

5. What judgment does Peter say will fall upon these clever but false teachers? (2 Peter 2:3,12,13,17)

Without a doubt, the greatest danger to the church has always been false teaching. It is a toxic poison that sneaks into the church, wreaking havoc, and causing eternal damage.

6. Read Matthew 7:15-20. What warning did Jesus give about the lethal threat of apostasy?

7. Paul issues a similar caution to the Ephesian elders in Acts 20:29-31. What four-word instruction does he give to the elders regarding false teachers?

8. Describe the lifestyle of the false teachers Peter references in 2 Peter 2:13-14.

In the pagan Roman society, acts of debauchery that occurred at night were allowed. However, even Roman unbelievers considered these behaviors inappropriate during the daytime. Notice that these false teachers were so consumed with their wicked living that they considered it a pleasure to participate in these acts, even during daylight hours. By their lifestyles, these false prophets were teaching that since we are free in Christ, we are also free to indulge the flesh. As Peter writes, he is not only warning against false teachers, but he is also admonishing believers against indulging the flesh.

9. What are some of the ways that we "indulge the flesh"?

But I say, walk by the Spirit, and you will not carry out the desire of the flesh.
Galatians 5:16

As you close out your study time today, ask God to show you any areas in your life where your profession and your practice do not match up. Surrender those places of indulgence to Him. As Tozer made clear, "We must surrender and God must have His way. His glory and our eternal welfare require that it be so."[8]

WEEK 5 · DAY TWO

There are days. And. Then. There. Are. Days.

This particular day had gone from bad to worse. And I was not handling "worse" well. To be clear, I wasn't dealing with the normal "bad day" type of things like a broken washer, a child with a stomach virus, or a dinner where the rolls were burnt and the roast was undercooked and tough. Those things, I could deal with. They just happen. But this was different. Disappointment and pain had found my address. My emotions were raw and my joy had gone on sabbatical.

Around lunchtime, I decided I needed to talk to someone who would understand what I was going through and to be completely honest, give me some sympathy. My husband was out of town and not in a place where he could talk so I shut the door to my office and called my parents. After a couple of rings, my dad answered the phone. Just hearing his voice unleashed waves of tears. In fact, I was crying so hard, I went into a closet in my office and shut the door so that no one could hear me as I uploaded my grief to my dad. He listened patiently for several minutes as I recounted what had been going on. And then, when I was finally quiet, he said five words, "Dead men feel no pain." In that instant, I received a much needed reminder of the words of 2 Corinthians 4:11-12, "For we who are alive are constantly being delivered over to death for Jesus' sake, so that the life of Jesus also may be manifested in our mortal flesh. So death works in us, but life in you."

It was time for a death. The death of my flesh.

The Greek word for "flesh" in the New Testament is *sarx*, a term that at times refers to the physical body. At other times, it refers to the sin nature. For the purposes of our study today, we are looking at the sin nature of our flesh.

Mark Bubeck gives an insightful description of the flesh:

> The flesh is a built-in law of failure, making it impossible for the natural man to please or serve God. It is a compulsive inner force inherited from man's fall, which expresses itself in general and specific rebellion against God and His righteousness. The flesh can never be reformed or improved. The only hope for escape from the law of the flesh is its total execution and replacement by a new life in the Lord Jesus Christ.[9]

Paul clarifies the components of the flesh in Romans 8:7-8, "…the mind set on the flesh is hostile toward God; for it does not subject itself to the law of God, for it is not even able to do so, and those who are in the flesh cannot please God."

1. What are the three defining elements of the flesh that Paul gives in Romans 8:7-8?

   •

   •

   •

2. Galatians 5:19-21 provides an overview of how the flesh is exposed. List the deeds that Paul says are evidence of the flesh.

The Adamic DNA of the natural man has within itself no ability to perform the things of God because as Paul explains, the "natural man does not accept the things of the Spirit of God, for they are foolishness to him; and he cannot understand them, because they are spiritually appraised" (1 Corinthians 2:14). In writing to the church at Ephesus, Paul offers additional understanding into the plight of man's condition before Christ, "Once you were dead because of your disobedience and your many sins. You used to live in sin, just like the rest of the world, obeying the devil—the commander of the powers in the unseen world. He is the spirit at work in the hearts of those who refuse to obey God. All of us used to live that way, following the passionate desires and inclinations of our sinful nature. By our very nature we were subject to God's anger, just like everyone else" (Ephesians 2:1-3 NLT).

3. Read Galatians 6:7-8. What are the consequences for those who live according to the flesh, never repenting of their sinful behavior?

But here is the great news! Just as birth into Adam's genealogical line gives man Adam's sin nature, birth into God's family gives man God's nature—a divine nature (2 Peter 1:4). The God nature is the goal for all who have experienced new birth, "Therefore if any man be in Christ, he is a new creature: old things are passed away; behold, all things are become new" (2 Corinthians 5:17).

And "new" really does mean "new". As we become a "new" creation in Christ, God does not reform or rehabilitate our flesh. There is nothing in our flesh worth rehabilitating (Romans 7:18). Instead, He introduces into our lives a "new" capacity of mind, heart and will. He gives us a new nature.

4. Read 1 Corinthians 2:12, 1 John 4:19, Romans 6:12, and Galatians 5:22-23. Describe the capabilities of the new nature we have in Christ.

So once we have trusted in Christ, we receive new life from the Spirit. But, our remaining sin, that part of our Adamic birthright that remains, hates the intrusion of this new nature. So the battle is on.

5. Read Galatians 5:17. How does Paul describe the conflict raging within believers?

The key to making the choice to walk in the Spirit is our mind-set—our beliefs and attitude of the heart that drive the course of our life.

Warren Wiersbe explains, "If the Holy Spirit controls the body, then we walk in the Spirit; but if the flesh controls the body, then we walk in the lusts (desires) of the flesh. The Spirit and the flesh have different appetites, and that is what creates the conflict."[10] This battle between flesh and spirit is a war within. From the moment we enter into new life in Christ, we are set free from enslavement to sin and given the capacity to live according to God's design. However, as long as we are in our physical bodies, our sinful flesh is still present and accounted for and surfaces in attempts to quench and grieve the Holy Spirit's influence in our lives. Take note though, the conflict is not in itself sinful; defeat is. God does not expect us to live in the absence of this internal conflict; but He does command us to be victorious in the fight.

6. Read Romans 8:12-13. Paul makes it clear that we have to keep on choosing to live according to our new identity in Christ. Why do we continually have to put to death our old sin nature habits?

The key to making the choice to walk in the Spirit is our mind-set—our beliefs and attitude of the heart that drive the course of our life. Consider Paul's instruction in Romans 8:5-6: "For those who are according to the flesh set their minds on the things of the flesh, but those who are according to the Spirit, the things of the Spirit. For the mind set on the flesh is death, but the mind set on the Spirit is life and peace."

What do you feed your mind-set that reflects the flesh? What do you feed your mind-set that reflects the Spirit?

There is an old illustration you may have heard before:

> A man had two dogs that he entered into dogfights. He placed a bet on a different one every time they fought each other and always won. Someone asked him, "How do you always know which dog will win?" He answered, "That is easy. The one I feed is the one who always wins."

Your flesh or your spirit? Whichever one you feed is the one that will win.

What changes do you need to make to cultivate a mind that is set on the Spirit?

> *Therefore if you have been raised up with Christ, keep seeking the things above, where Christ is, seated at the right hand of God. Set your mind on the things above, not on the things that are on earth.*
> Colossians 3:1-2

The battle had been hard fought on both sides. It was February 16, 1862, and for five days more than 13,000 Confederate soldiers had been defending Fort Donelson on the Cumberland River outside the northwestern Tennessee town of Dover near the Tennessee-Kentucky border. A relatively unproven Union leader, General Ulysses S. Grant, led three divisions of the Union Army, totaling almost 25,000 men in the battle. That morning, when it became apparent that the Confederate Army was surrounded, Confederate Brigadier General Simon Buckner, a pre-war friend of Grant's, sent a note to the Union general to request a truce and inquire about the terms of surrender. Grant's now famous reply was, "No terms except unconditional and immediate surrender can be accepted."

Later that day, Buckner and Grant met to work out the details of what was, to that point, the greatest military surrender in American history. Under the conditions of unconditional surrender, the Confederate soldiers were to stack their guns on the banks of the Cumberland and board boats headed for Northern prisons. No discussion. No compromise. And with that, the Battle of Fort Donelson was over, earning Grant the nickname "Unconditional Surrender" Grant.[11]

In terms of the language of war, unconditional surrender means that no guarantees are given to the surrendering party. They are completely at the mercy of their conquering foe.

Our flesh opposes the idea of unconditional surrender at every turn. How many times have we lied our way through "I Surrender All" when we actually had no intent to "freely give" Him our all? We want the mercy of God, but still want to retain our self-sufficient independence. And so we try to tuck our sin away in the deep recesses of our heart, in some type of ludicrous attempt to hide it from God. But, not only is God totally aware of every area of our flesh that is still alive and kicking, someone else also takes notice. The enemy is on the prowl, looking for any area of sin still lurking in the believer's heart. And any unsurrendered area we tolerate will leave us vulnerable for a future attack. No one knew that better than Peter.

Read Luke 22:31-34.

1. What does Jesus tell Peter in verse 31?

In the Greek, the word "you" in verse 31 is plural. Satan had demanded to put a target on the backs of all of the disciples, but Peter, the leader of the bunch, is obviously going to be singled out. Notice that Satan does not say, "please" to God; he demands permission from the Sovereign. We see this same tactic when he approaches God about Job (Job 1:9-12; Job 2:4-6).

Two implications are important for us to let sink in. First, Satan has power in the world.

2. Read John 16:11. What does Jesus call Satan?

The second implication is that Satan's power has a permit from God. Satan is subordinate and cannot go after a believer without God granting him permission. I am pretty sure I can hear the question you are asking, "Why would God give the enemy what he demands?" And I believe the answer is that it is for our good and His glory.

John Piper gives insight that will further our understanding:

> I picture God as an omniscient general whose aim is to fight and win the war in the way that will bring him most glory for his magnificent, strategic wisdom and power. Instead of steam rolling over the enemy all at once, he combines strategic advances and retreats that allow the enemy some illusion of success and brings out all their arrogance and hate for the general, so that it can be seen for what it is. In his wisdom the general knows when the end should come. He will give way for a time to allow the enemy to rage in defiance, and then when sin is seen for all that it is, he will close in and destroy the enemy in such a way that none can doubt the wisdom and glory and power of the general.[12]

3. By what name does Jesus call Peter in verse 31?

When Jesus uses the disciple's pre-Christ name twice instead of his new, promise-filled name, He does so to get his attention. The *New International Commentary on the New Testament* notes:

> By addressing Peter as 'Simon, Simon' (with the repetition), the Saviour calls upon him to realize the seriousness of the matter which He is going to discuss. And by calling him 'Simon' instead of 'Peter,' Jesus reminds him of his human weakness...[13]

Satan planned to take advantage of the weakness of Peter's sin nature for the sake of his demonic plan. The visual picture of "sifting" that Jesus used with Peter was familiar. Israel was an agricultural society, so even though Peter was a fisherman, he knew well the grain-sifting process. Piles of grain would be shoveled onto a sifter, or sieve. Workers would then vigorously shake the sieve, causing all dirt and chaff to fall through the screen to the ground until only the pure kernels of grain remained. Sifting was a purification process.

What in particular was Peter's issue? Let's back up a few verses to get some insight. After they finished the Passover meal, Jesus announced to the disciples that one of them was going to betray him. Their discussion regarding who the traitor could possibly be quickly turned into an argument over which one of them was the greatest. (See Luke 22:21-24.)

And Peter, the leader, is right there in the middle of the dispute and apparently comes out ahead. Even after Jesus' somber words directed at him in verses 31-32, Peter refuses to believe that he would succumb to Satan's plan. His issue? Pride.

4. How does Peter respond to Jesus? (v. 33)

Can't you just hear it in his voice? "I'm ready." "Let's do this thing." "You have already told me what eternity has in store." "I am willing to die." "What harm can a little sifting do?" The old self-reliant, prideful Peter had no idea what he was about to face.

Jesus then warned Peter that "the rooster will not crow today until you have denied three times that you know me." And as we read in verses 54-62, that is exactly what happened. With the crowing of the rooster, Peter was cut to the core of his being by the realization of his failure and he went out and wept bitterly. As his tears fell, his healing began.

Let's go back to examine what Jesus says to Peter after he told him what Satan had demanded.

5. What does Jesus tell Peter in verse 32?

The bottom line is that Jesus has the upper hand in this fight. Satan may be the adversary, but Jesus is the Intercessor and Advocate. Satan's plan was destruction; Jesus' goal was restoration. And although Peter would experience temporary failure, he would ultimately be restored to even greater usefulness in the kingdom (John 21). Jesus was not going to let Peter fall through the sieve.

The plan Satan devised to destroy Peter's faith instead worked to perfect him as the pride in Peter was replaced with the nature of Christ.

Peter's area of vulnerability was pride. What is yours? STOP. Don't just keep on reading. Answer the question (either in your mind or make a note in the margin). Get it out there with God. Repent. Truth that is not obeyed is not only useless, but it hardens the heart. It is time for an unconditional surrender. The best defense we have before Satan is to keep a pure heart with the Father.

...so that no advantage would be taken of us by Satan,
for we are not ignorant of his schemes.
2 Corinthians 2:11

WEEK 5 · DAY FOUR

Warren Wiersbe writes, "Sooner or later every believer discovers that the Christian life is a battleground, not a playground, and that he faces an enemy that is much stronger than he is—apart from the Lord."[14] From the moment you made the decision to follow Christ, you enlisted in His army and became a soldier in battle for spiritual dominion that began with Adam and Eve. The enemy has targeted you for annihilation and he does not play around; every minute of every day, it is "war on". Bob Sorge explains the way Satan devises his battle plan:

> The nature of the enemy's warfare in your life is to cause you to become discouraged and to cast away your confidence. Not that you would necessarily discard your salvation, but you could give up your hope of God's deliverance. The enemy wants to numb you into a coping kind of Christianity that has given up hope of seeing God's resurrection power.[15]

We must not settle for a "coping kind of Christianity" that causes the world to see Christians as those who live powerless lives without hope, who are numb to the promises of God, who live, in the words of Teddy Roosevelt, "in that gray twilight that knows neither victory nor defeat."[16] It is time for us to be fully engaged in the battle. And to do that, we need to have a firm grasp on the Battle Basics.

Read Ephesians 6:10-14a.

In these verses Paul gives us the basics of the battle: Position, Powers, Place, Posture. Let's look at these one at a time.

Position

From 1775-1783, our ancestors fought the Revolutionary War that would free us from the tyranny of the British Empire. Although you and I have never fired a shot at a British soldier, we enjoy the position we have as free Americans today because they won the victory for us. Our freedom is a direct result of their sacrifice.

In the same way, our position in the spiritual battle we are in has also been won. Jesus died for our freedom more than 2000 years ago.

1. Take another look at Colossians 2:15. What happened as a result of Christ's death?

The very thing that appeared to seal Christ's demise became His tool of triumph. In a divine plot twist, the emblem of suffering and shame by which the demonic hosts believed they had defeated Christ, was turned on them as the instrument of their humiliating conquest. Jesus proved once and for all that all power and authority in the universe and beyond belongs to Him.

2. Read Romans 8:37. Who are we in Christ?

Believers have three enemies: the world, the flesh, and the devil. These enemies are leftovers from our old life (Ephesians 2:1-3) and although Christ has delivered us from them, they still attack us. When that happens, it is paramount for us to understand that we are not fighting *for* victory; we are fighting *from* victory. God does not need us to defeat the devil; we simply need to enforce the victory Christ has already won. Our position in the fight is victory ground. In Christ's power, we are invincible.

> *It is paramount for us to understand that we are not fighting for victory; we are fighting from victory.*

3. James 4:7 tells us how to enforce the victory we have in Christ. What are we commanded to do?

-
-

"Submit" is a military word that means to "rank under". It refers to coming under the sovereign authority of God, which means obeying His Word and denying self (Luke 9:23). "Resist" is also a military metaphor that urges us to stand in our position of victory against the scheming attacks of the enemy.[17]

4. How does your understanding of your position in Christ help you in the daily battle? Give a personal example.

Powers

Satan would like nothing more than to keep us in a distorted battle against the wrong enemies: people here on earth. If he can make us think that our battle is in the physical world with family members, friends, work associates, church members, and political leaders, he keeps us distracted from our real foes. But Paul makes it clear, "For we wrestle not against flesh and blood, but against principalities, against powers, against the rulers of the darkness of this world, against spiritual wickedness in high places" (Ephesians 6:12 KJV).

We battle a supernatural, angelic foe who fell from heaven and took a third of the angels with him with the goal of defeating us in every area.

Charles Hodge, in his commentary on Ephesians, provides some insight into the spiritual opposition that Paul is writing about in Ephesians 6:12:

> The whole context, however, shows that the design of the apostle is to present the formidable character of our adversaries in the most impressive point of view. Others suppose that Paul means to refer to the former, and not to the present residence of these exalted beings. They are fallen angels, who once dwelt in heaven. But his is obviously inconsistent with the natural meaning of his words. He speaks of them as in heaven. It is better to take the word heaven in a wised sense. It is very often used antithetically to the word earth. "Heaven and earth," include the whole universe. All intelligent beings are terrestrial or celestial. Of the latter class some are good and some are bad, as of the angels some are holy and some are unholy. These principalities and potentates, these rulers and spirits of wickedness, are no earthly magnates, they belong to the order of celestial intelligences, and therefore are the more to be dreaded, and something more than human strength and earthly armour is required for the conflict to which the apostle refers.[18]

An uninformed soldier is a soldier in peril. It is important for us to understand who our opponent is in the battle. Paul explains Satan's system in Ephesians 6:12.

Principalities – The Greek word for "principalities" is *arche,* which means chief or ruler.[19] Similar to generals, these are the most powerful beings in Satan's command. They issue assignments, plot strategies, and position lesser demonic forces in specific areas. 2 Corinthians 4:3-4 tells us that their main goal is to keep people from coming to know Christ as Savior and Lord.

Powers – The word "powers" is the Greek noun, *exousia,* and means one who possesses authority or influence.[20] These fallen angels have influence over a state, province, or territory in a country and must be dealt with to open up the gospel in those areas. Satan is not omnipresent, but these powers are an extension of his evil character. Daniel 10:12-13 tells us of the spiritual ruler who had authority over the ancient nation of Persia and whose power was broken by the archangel Michael's prevailing strength and the persevering prayers of Daniel.

Rulers of the Darkness of the World – These are lesser spirits that operate within the context of Satan's organization. Some commentators believe these spirits propagate false teaching and the occult.

Spiritual Wickedness in High Places – These wicked spirits dwell in high places. The Greek word for "high places" is translated *epouranios* and refers to the dwelling place of God as well as the abode of angels and evil spirits. Vine's dictionary says *epouranios,* also translated "heavenly places", is a reference to the sphere of activity or existence that is above, in contrast to that of the earth.[21] Most commentaries explain that the spiritual wickedness is describing demons, devils or evil spirits.

The entire human race is under vicious attack by powerful invisible rulers of darkness and highly placed demonic agents of spiritual wickedness. But only believers are capable of understanding the true nature of the conflict and the reality of the warfare.

5. How can a correct view of satanic opposition impact your "flesh and blood" relational struggles?

Place

Paul tells us that the battle with Satan and his demonic creatures is in the "heavenly places". Where are these places located? In the spiritual realm. As Tony Evans explains, "Whatever has gone on, is going on, or will go on in your visible, physical world is rooted in the invisible, spiritual realm."[22] Try as we may, we cannot overcome in the physical world, with physical means, what is taking place in the spiritual world.

6. Read Ephesians 1:3. What does Paul tell us about the spiritual realm?

Everything God has done for us, our blessings and our victory, is deposited in an account in the spiritual realm with our name on it. We just need to access them through faith, believing our Commander-in-Chief.

Posture

Three times in Ephesians 6:10-14a, Paul communicates to us our posture for the battle. It is to stand. And not only are we to stand, we are to put on our armor and stand firm. Hold our ground. Immovable. Unyielding.

Regardless of the circumstances of "the evil day," when the war intensifies, we are to stand resisting, persevering, knowing that in the strength of Christ our victory has already been secured. When we continue to stand in the face of the situations the enemy designed for our defeat and demise, he will flee.

Soldier of God, it is time to stand!

I am a soldier in the army of my God.
The Lord Jesus Christ is my Commanding Officer.
The Holy Scripture is my code of conduct.
Faith, prayer and the Word are my weapons of warfare.
I have been taught by the Holy Spirit, trained by experience, tried by adversity and tested by fire.

I am a volunteer in this army, and I am enlisted for eternity.
I will not get out, sell out, be talked out or pushed out.
I am faithful, reliable, capable and dependable.
If my God needs me, I am there. I am a soldier.

I am not a baby. I do not need to be pampered, petted, primed up, pumped up,
picked up, or pepped up. I am a soldier.
No one has to call me, remind me, write me, visit me, entice me or lure me. I am a soldier. I am not a wimp. I am in place, saluting my King, obeying His orders, praising His name and building

His kingdom! No one has to send me flowers, gifts, food, cards or candy, or give me handouts. I do not need to be cuddled, cradled, cared for or catered to. I am committed. I cannot have my feelings hurt bad enough to turn me around. I cannot be discouraged enough to turn me aside. I cannot lose enough to cause me to quit.

When Jesus called me into this army, I had nothing. If I end up with nothing,
I will still come out ahead. I will win. My God has and will continue to supply all
of my need. I am more than a conqueror. I will always triumph. I can do all things through Christ
The devil cannot defeat me.
People cannot disillusion me. Weather cannot weary me.
Sickness cannot stop me. Battles cannot beat me.
Money cannot buy me.
Governments cannot silence me, and hell cannot handle me.
I am a soldier.

Even death cannot destroy me. For when my Commander calls me from His battlefield, He will promote me to captain and then allow me to rule with Him. I am a soldier in the army, and I'm marching claiming victory. I will not give up. I will not turn around. I am a soldier, marching heaven-bound. Here I Stand! Will you stand with me?[23]

~ Anonymous

WEEK 5 · DAY FIVE

The Screwtape Letters, a fictional work by C.S. Lewis, is a compilation of 31 letters written by a senior demon named Screwtape to his nephew, Wormwood. Wormwood's job is to keep his subject, a newly converted believer, under spiritual attack. As the young man learns to resist the attacks, Screwtape writes in frustration to Wormwood, lamenting the lack of progress the junior demon is making:

> For as things are, your man has now discovered the dangerous truth that these attacks don't last forever; consequently you cannot use again what is, after all, our best weapon – the belief of ignorant humans, that there is no hope of getting rid of us except by yielding.[24]

As we saw yesterday, victory is ours when we refuse to yield and stand firm in the spiritual realm against the schemes of the enemy. And what enables us to stand firm? As Paul tells us, "Put on the full armor of God, so that you will be able to stand firm against the schemes of the devil" (Ephesians 6:11). Satan wants us to believe the lie that we have "no hope of getting rid" of his assaults. The truth is that when we are dressed in the full armor of God, we will be able to hold our ground and fend off the attacks that come our way.

Over the next six days, we will look in detail at each piece of the armor that God has provided for us. The pieces of the armor are powerful tools that will enable us to withstand and overcome the onslaughts of Satan. Paul was well acquainted with every detail of a Roman soldier's wardrobe as he had spent somewhere between five to six years in prison chained next to a soldier. In fact, he was in a Roman prison at the time he was writing the letter to the church at Ephesus. So the spiritual armor he writes about in Ephesians 6 is patterned after the armor and weapons used by a Roman soldier in Paul's day.

The Belt of Truth

The first piece of the armor Paul names in Ephesians 6:14-18 is the belt of truth. "Stand firm therefore, having girded your loins with truth" (v. 14).

A Roman soldier's complete marching armor weighed about 66 pounds. The belt was the first part of the armor the soldier put on and it secured the other pieces of his armor. Similar to a holster and worn around his midsection, this leather belt stabilized his breastplate as well as provided an organized place to hang his sword, dagger, and other tools. When a soldier had his belt on, it indicated that he was ready for action, since he would only loosen his belt when he was off duty.

Under his armor, the soldier wore a tunic, a garment draped loosely over his body. Since most combat was hand-to-hand, a loose tunic was a potential hindrance and even a danger. When the battle cry sounded, the soldier would gather up his tunic and tuck it into his belt, allowing for free range of motion in combat. This gathering up process was called *girding* and was essential to the soldier being prepared to do battle.[25]

1. What does Paul say that we should gird ourselves with?

John MacArthur makes this insightful observation:

> I believe that being girded ... with truth primarily has to do with the self–discipline of total commitment. It is the committed Christian, just as it is the committed soldier and the committed athlete, who is prepared. Winning in war and in sports is often said to be the direct result of desire that leads to careful preparation and maximum effort. It is the army or the team who wants most to win who is most likely to do so—even against great odds...To be content with mediocrity, lethargy, indifference, and half–heartedness is to fail to be armored with the belt of God's truth and to leave oneself exposed to Satan's schemes.[26]

Girding ourselves with the belt of truth requires disciplined action on our part. Although Satan's power was broken on the cross (Hebrews 2:14-15), he is the ruler of this world and can still cause us harm. Louie Giglio explains this tension, "We live in the great expanse of time and space between two points: the cross and the final work of Jesus in the end times when everything is made right... Satan has been defeated, yet he is still dangerous."[27] So, we must be prepared for whatever he will throw our way. Since his first attack in the Garden, Satan has been peddling deception (John 8:44). Liar is his name; deceit is his game. Therefore, truth is a critical component for every believer in the battle. Without it, we are not prepared to stand firm and fight.

We are living in a postmodern age when there is no single defining source for truth and reality beyond individual preference. It is a "Do what you want, like what you do" society where the enemy has a heyday twisting and perverting the truth.

2. What are some ways you have seen truth corrupted just this week? (You may have seen truth corrupted in the news, on social media, in a book, or heard it corrupted in a song.) Share a specific instance.

The word *truth* in Ephesians 6:14 means candor, sincerity, and truthfulness. Paul explained absolute truth to the Ephesian believers earlier in his letter.

3. Read Ephesians 4:21. Where does "truth" come from?

Truth is a Person. Truth flows right from Jesus Christ, the King of the Universe. As the second person in the Trinity, He is the Creator of all things. So all truth finds its source in Jesus. This fact is firmly established by the prophet Isaiah. Paul's resource is not only the Roman armor, but also the fulfillment of Isaiah's prophecy of Christ as the divine warrior who came to rescue God's people:

> ...truth has stumbled in the public squares, and uprightness cannot enter. Truth is lacking...The Lord saw it, and it displeased him...then his own arm brought him salvation...He put on righteousness as a breastplate, and a helmet of salvation on his head; he put on garments of vengeance for clothing, and wrapped himself in zeal as a cloak (Isaiah 59:14-17).

Truth is not found in notions or theories, truth is found in the person of Jesus Christ, the living embodiment of the truth. Our culture has relegated truth to an individually defined concept. "That may be true for you, but not for me" implies that truth is up for a vote. If ten million people believe a lie, it is still a lie. Just a thought–if truth had stumbled in the public squares in Isaiah's day, it is flat on its face in the day in which we live. God's answer, then and now, is for Jesus to be our absolute default in every circumstance, action, and response. He must have the final say in our lives.

4. Read John 17:17. What "truth" is being referred to in "belt of truth"?

Truth is what God says. "Sanctify them in the truth; Your Word is truth" (John 17:17). As a teenager, I heard Jack Taylor preach a sermon on the truth of God's Word. Over and over again, he said, "Truth is what God says." That one statement has echoed through my life for decades. We must know and be able to share the truth of God's Word. To do that, we must live in God's Word, and His Word must live in us.

5. Read John 8:31-32. Why do you think that Satan would want to keep us from God's Word?

Truth sets us free. The opposite of freedom is bondage and slavery. No one wants to live that way. In John 8:38, Jesus drives His point in deeper, "If the Son sets you free, you will be free indeed." *Free indeed* is freedom in its fullest measure. Through Jesus we are free from the condemnation of sin and the domination of sin. When our sins are forgiven and we enter into a new life in Christ, we are freed from the condemnation of sin because of the Christ's redemptive act at Calvary. And as new creations, we are free from the domination of sin as we daily throw off the old man and put on the new. But to be clear, it is a choice we make. God will not force us to put on the belt of truth. But as we do, He will enable us to fight against the enemy's clever strategies. And those strategies are clever.

> *Truth is not found in notions or theories, truth is found in the person of Jesus Christ, the living embodiment of the truth.*

Satan will plant wrong thoughts in our minds that contradict the truth of God (2 Corinthians 10:5). It could be something as simple as a friend's opinion or your own self-generated thoughts. And take careful note–Satan will let you mix a little of God's truth with his distorted message because he knows the damage twisted truth can do. Anything, anything, anything that doesn't align 100% with God's Word must be taken captive to the obedience of Jesus Christ.

Is there any area in your life where you are being deceived? Have you fallen for a lie that Satan has planted in your mind? Have you taken off your Belt of Truth?

Search me, O God, and know my heart; Try me and know my anxious thoughts;
And see if there be any hurtful way in me, And lead me in the everlasting way.
Psalm 139:23-24

Remember, we are at war, but we don't fight with human weapons. The weapons of our warfare are divinely made to resist the enemy of our souls (2 Corinthians 10:3-4). The kingdom of darkness is our opponent, and we are fighting for the truth. We are fighting for freedom. We are engaged in war. Put on your belt of truth and let's go!

The Right Way

Take Up the Full Armor

This life therefore is not righteousness, but growth in righteousness, not health, but healing,
not being but becoming, not rest but exercise. We are not yet what we shall be, but we are growing
toward it, the process is not yet finished, but it is going on, this is not the end, but it is the road.
All does not yet gleam in glory, but all is being purified.[1]
~Martin Luther

In 2 Peter 2:15-16, Peter draws from the Old Testament story of Balaam as a comparison to the false teachers who were trying to lead Christians astray. Peter notes that these false teachers were forsaking "the right way" and like Balaam loved the "wages of unrighteousness." (For more about Balaam and his talking donkey read Numbers 22-24.) In verse 17, Peter concludes that these false teachers are "springs without water and mists driven by a storm." These teachers of error had no substance of truth in their message and were making empty promises to entice others to follow them.

As we saw last week, the belt of truth is the first piece of the spiritual armor because we have to *know* the truth before we can *apply* the truth. That is where righteousness comes in. It is putting what we know into practice.

The Right Way

WEEK 6 · DAY ONE

The Breastplate of Righteousness

Remember that as Paul is writing his instructions regarding the spiritual armor, he is in a Roman prison cell. It is likely that he can see a Roman soldier through the bars of his cell and is able to contemplate in detail each piece of the soldier's armor. After the belt of truth, Paul tells us that the next piece of armor is the breastplate of righteousness and instructs us to put it on (Ephesians 6:14). Truth comes before righteousness because without truth, there is no righteousness.

The breastplate was a critical part of the Roman soldier's armor. It was a sturdy sleeveless piece of armor usually made of bronze or chain mail that covered the soldier's whole torso and provided protection for "the heart, lungs, intestines, and other vital organs."[2] Without his breastplate in place, a soldier would be vulnerable to death, as any attack could go straight to his heart and instantly become fatal. However, with a strong breastplate on, the very same assaults were futile and unsuccessful, as blows just ricocheted off of the armor.

In Hebrew thought, the heart represented three areas: the mind, the will, and the bowels (the seat of the emotions).[3] The mind and the emotions are the two areas where Satan most fiercely attacks believers. As Proverbs 4:23 states, "Watch over your heart with all diligence, for from it flow the springs of life." What protects our hearts from the attack of the enemy? The breastplate of righteousness!

In 1 Kings 22, we see an example of just how important the breastplate was in battle. King Ahab was a cowardly, evil king who "did evil in the sight of the Lord more than all who were before him" (1 Kings 16:30). This king of Israel, among many other terrible acts, allowed Naboth of Jezreeel to be killed just because he coveted the Jezreelite's vineyard (1 Kings 21). In 1 Kings 22, the prophet Micaiah prophesied that Ahab would die in a battle against the King Aram of Ramoth-Gilead. So when he went to war, Ahab decided to disguise himself, while his ally, King Jehoshaphat of Judah, wore his own royal robes.

King Aram had ordered his captains to only fight King Ahab. When they saw King Jehoshaphat in his kingly attire, they said:

> 'It is surely the king of Israel.' So they turned to fight against him; and Jehoshaphat cried out. When the captains of the chariots saw that it was not the king of Israel, they turned back from pursuing him. But a certain man drew his bow and unknowingly struck the king of Israel between the scale armor and the breastplate… at evening he died; the blood from the wound had flowed into the bottom of the chariot (1 Kings 22: 32-35 NRSV).

The lack of protection caused by an opening in Ahab's armor allowed the arrow to penetrate right through him. Justice served for a life defined by wickedness, wouldn't you say?

1. Read Isaiah 59:1-2. What is it that separates us from God, causing Him to withhold His protection?

Iniquities and sins are actions and thoughts that are contrary to God's laws. Since they are in conflict with the holy character of God, we cut ourselves off from Him and His protection if we choose the path of sin.

2. Read Jeremiah 5:25. Describe in a practical way what sin and iniquity do to us.

3. Read Proverbs 11:4. What does righteousness deliver us from?

Without righteousness, we are vulnerable. With righteousness—just as with a breastplate—the otherwise fatal attacks of our enemy are foiled.

4. What is righteousness? After reading Psalm 119:172, 1 John 3:4, and 1 Corinthians 15:34, define righteousness.

Romans 3:10 makes it clear, "There is none righteous, not even one" and Isaiah 64:6 tells us that "all our righteous deeds are like a filthy garment." So since righteousness delivers from death, and our individual level of righteousness is the equivalent of "filthy rags"—whose righteousness are we dependent upon?

5. Read Jeremiah 23:6. Who does the prophet say is our righteousness?

6. Consider the words of the Psalmist in Psalm 5:8; 23:3; 24:5; and 71:16. What does he tell us about righteousness?

Tony Evans explains that there are two sides to righteousness, "the being side and the doing side."[4] 2 Corinthians 5:21 explains the "being side" of righteousness.

7a. Read 2 Corinthians 5:21. What did we receive because of Christ?

7b. What did Christ receive on our behalf?

Evans gives insight into the believer's position in Christ:

> Righteousness has been imputed to everyone who has trusted in Jesus Christ for the forgiveness of their sins. When we talk about salvation, we often think of this idea of the forgiveness of sins. While this is one thing that happens at the moment of salvation, it is not the only thing. In fact, forgiveness on its own is not enough to get a person into heaven. God did more than forgive our sins through Jesus Christ. He also imputed, or credited to our account, the righteousness of Jesus Christ... God not only removed the stain of your sin when you trusted in Jesus Christ but also replaced that stain with the righteous standard of Christ. So now when God looks at you, He sees you as equal to His Son. He doesn't just see someone who has been forgiven of his or her sins; He sees someone who has kept the full standard of righteousness.[5]

Once we are saved, nothing can change our righteous standing before God. But since Satan cannot strip away our imputed righteousness, he will do everything he can to try to keep us from living it out. Living it out is the "doing" part of our righteousness.

8. Read Psalm 119:172 again. How do we live righteous lives?

John MacArthur expounds on the believer's practice of righteousness:

> To put on the breastplate of righteousness is to live in daily, moment-by-moment obedience to our heavenly Father. This part of God's armor is holy living, for which God supplies the standard and the power but for which we must supply the willingness. God Himself puts on our imputed righteousness, but we must put on our practical righteousness.[6]

In Ephesians 4:24, Paul explains that we are to "put on the new self, which in *the likeness of* God has been created in righteousness and holiness of the truth." And as new creatures, we are to walk in a new way. As Paul writes, "for you were formerly darkness, but now you are Light in the Lord; walk as children of Light (for the fruit of the Light *consists* in all goodness and righteousness and truth)" (Ephesians 5:8-9). As we walk in this world as new creatures in Christ, we will be growing in conformity to God's standard of holiness as revealed in His Word.

9. What areas do you struggle with that keep you from walking in righteousness?

Since Satan knows he cannot take away our righteous standing before God, he will scheme to get us to sin, causing a breach between our position of righteousness and our practice of righteousness. Sin breaks our fellowship with God and makes us spiritually unproductive. If there is a gap between our profession of Christ and our practice, Satan will then come against us with accusations to mire us down in the muck of our sin.

10. When we do sin, what does 1 John 1:9 tell us to do?

We confess our sin and then put our breastplate of righteousness back on, once again "dressed in His righteousness alone, faultless to stand before the throne."[7]

I love to hike. My husband and I take at least one week a year and hike in the mountains. We enjoy everything about the experience. Beauty. Nature. Silence. Togetherness. The times we spend on the trails are treasured moments. But it wasn't always so. When we first married, my husband had considerable experience hiking. Me? I am sure I had walked around the block a couple of times, but that was the extent of my hiking resume. After we had been married a few months, we took a weekend trip to the mountains. My plans were to observe the mountains from the vista of the shopping malls. His plans were to really see the mountains. On foot. Being new at this communication thing, we neglected to discuss our individual goals prior to the weekend. Once we got there and realized that we had opposing plans, we worked out a compromise. We would do a little shopping and a little hiking.

The only problem was that I had not packed hiking boots (because who even owns a pair to walk around the block?), nor had I packed tennis shoes. The only shoes I had with me were loafers, which really were in style at the time, and would look great with the pleated skirt and knee socks I choose to wear on my first real hiking adventure. (In all fairness to my wonderful husband, I am pretty sure that he suggested perhaps I wear something different to no avail. Because in my mind, cute trumped practical.)

Knowing nothing at the time about trailheads, I did not even glance at the posted information when we arrived at the trail and had no idea that we were actually undertaking a hike with a rating of "moderately strenuous". Neither did I have any idea that the hike was five and half miles round trip and would take more than three hours to complete. Honestly, I thought we would be in and out and back at the mall in less than an hour.

Imagine my surprise as we just kept on walking and walking and walking. Uphill. Regularly stumping my toes on rocks and roots. By the time we got to the destination waterfall, my feet were hurting so badly, I didn't even want to see it. And the realization that I was only halfway through our "adventure" did nothing to help my mood or my feet. And believe it or not the downhill trip was harder on my feet than the uphill. Loafers have no traction and I slipped and tripped several times just trying to get my bruised and aching feet back to the car. And when I did, I was pretty determined that I would never hike again.

Wearing the right shoes makes a huge difference whether you are hiking a trail, playing a sport, or fighting a battle. I now have a great pair of hiking boots (which my husband bought for me), and my feet have long forgotten that first miserable hiking venture. The right shoes really make all the difference. So it probably won't surprise you that the next piece of armor we need to experience victory involves shoes—shoes of peace.

The Shoes of Peace

"and having shod your feet with the preparation of the gospel of peace..."
Ephesians 6:15

A Roman soldier's shoes were called *caliga* and were a sturdy half boot with open toes. A soldier's life could depend upon his shoes. In war, he had to march over all kinds of terrain. Along the way, there might be rocks or other objects that he would have to negotiate that could cut his feet. If he did not have excellent footwear, he would be useless for battle by the time he got to the field.[8] In addition to providing protection for his feet, the caliga were also designed to give him traction. The shoes had small nails protruding from the bottom to dig into the ground so that the soldier would not slip and fall during the fight.[9]

In the same way, believers must wear appropriate footwear in spiritual battles. Having sturdy shoes speaks to our preparation for the battle, our readiness to stand firm against the enemy. F.F. Bruce writes, "Those who must at all costs stand their ground need to have a secure footing; in the spiritual conflict, this is supplied by the gospel, appropriated and proclaimed."[10]

You cannot put on the boots of the gospel of peace until you've appropriated the gospel personally. Appropriating the gospel personally begins with repentance from sin and faith in Christ alone for salvation.

1. Jesus summarized the gospel in Mark 1:15. What did he say?

So the critical question is, "Have you repented of your sins and believed in Jesus Christ as your Savior and Lord?" You cannot put on the shoes of peace unless you have a personal relationship with the Prince of Peace. If this is not a settled issue in your life, please do not read another word without committing your life to him. (See Appendix, "How to Become a Christian.")

But appropriating peace is not just a one-time event at the time of our salvation. In Colossians 3:15, Paul writes, "Let the peace of Christ rule in your hearts, to which indeed you were called in one body; and be thankful." A lack of spiritual faithfulness, fear, and guilt are just some of the things that can trip us up and cause us to lose our peace.

2. What is peace? Write your own definition.

The Greek word translated as "peace" is *eirene* and is the equivalent to the Hebrew word you are probably more familiar with, *shalom*. Tony Evans notes that *eirene* "embodies completeness, wholeness, and an inner resting of the soul that does not fluctuate because of outside influences."[11]

3. What does it look like when the peace of Christ is ruling in our lives?

4. How do our lives appear when His peace is not reigning in our lives?

God's peace is not tied to our circumstances. God's peace allows us to be at rest regardless of our circumstances. Peace is not found in the absence of problems; real peace is found in the presence of God.

5. How does Paul describe peace in Philippians 4:7?

6. Think of a time when you have experienced that kind of peace. What was that like?

Isaiah gives us the instructions for strapping on the shoes of peace, "You will keep him in perfect peace, Whose mind is stayed on You, Because he trusts in You" (Isaiah 26:3 NKJV).

7. Describe what it means to trust in God.

8. What are some scriptures that help you to "stay" your mind on Christ when you are in the middle of a spiritual battle?

Here is the deal. We can put on the belt of truth to stand against Satan's deceptive schemes and the breastplate of righteousness to fend off his accusations, but we won't be battle ready if we can't keep our footing in the fight. The shoes of peace are what keep us upright and steady when the enemy tries to knock us off of our feet.

One last thing. One of the ways we become more firmly established is by sharing our faith. Every day we are with people who do not know what it means to have the peace of God in their lives. Ask God for an opportunity to Share Jesus with someone this week. And as you do, your shoes will dig in deeper into our "foundation...Jesus Christ" (1 Corinthians 3:11).

Spartan soldiers were among the mightiest, bravest, and best warriors history has ever known. Literally, from the day they were born, Spartan boys were trained to become warriors. Those who survived infancy and early childhood training were taken from their families at the age of seven to begin formal battlefield training. As a result, Sparta became one of the most powerful cities in Ancient Greece, and it all came down to their army. They were feared throughout the ancient world. In their home city of Sparta, there were no walls, as the Spartans were convinced their warriors were strong enough to defeat any force that would come against them. Interestingly enough, Sparta was the only city in Ancient Greece that Alexander the Great never conquered.

Charles Spurgeon writes:

> Like the Spartans, every Christian is born a warrior. It is his destiny to be assaulted; it is his duty to attack. Part of his life will be occupied with defensive warfare. He will have to defend earnestly the faith once delivered to the saints. He will have to resist the devil, he will have to stand against all his wiles, and having done all, still to stand. He will, however, be but a sorry Christian if he acts only on the defensive. He must be one who goes against his foes, as well as stands still to receive their advance. He must be able to say with David, "I come against you in the name of the LORD of hosts, the God of the armies of Israel whom you have defied."[12]

So far, we have examined three pieces of the armor that the Christian warrior must wear. We have seen the belt of truth that allows us to stand against the enemy's lies, the breastplate of righteousness that protects our hearts when Satan attacks, and the shoes of peace that keep us steady in the battle. The fourth piece of armor is the shield of faith.

The Shield of Faith

Paul gives the next instruction on the spiritual armor that will help us to stand firm in warfare:

> *…in addition to all, taking up the shield of faith with which you will be*
> *able to extinguish all the flaming arrows of the evil one.*
> Ephesians 6:16

Roman soldiers had two kinds of shields. They had a small shield that fit on one arm and could easily be maneuvered to ward off the enemy's sword in man-to-man combat. The second shield, called a *thureos*, was a larger shield about four feet high by two and a half feet wide. Soldiers who carried these were on the front lines and would stand side-by-side to form a wall of defense that could extend as long as a mile. The *thureos* is the shield that Paul is referring to in Ephesians 6:16. These large shields were made of wood, covered with leather, and bound with iron. As the soldiers would stand shield to shield, they would be protected from the enemy's flaming arrows.[13]

Paul tells us that faith is our shield. D. Martyn Lloyd-Jones says, "Faith here means the ability to apply quickly what we believe so as to repel everything the devil does or attempts to do to us."[14] In his first letter, Peter gives similar instruction to the persecuted believers. After warning them that their adversary, the devil, was on the prowl to devour them, Peter adds, "But resist him, firm in your faith…." (1 Peter 5:9). The shield of faith enables the believer to live a life of victory in an atmosphere of attack as it quenches every fiery dart the devil hurls at us.

1. Read 1 John 5:4. How do we overcome the world and the god of this world (2 Corinthians 4:4)?

Faith is our victory! This faith John writes about is not the one time faith we exercised when we initially came to Christ; it is the day-by-day, moment-by-moment faith in the life of Jesus present in us. Today. This very moment.

2. Read Hebrews 11:1 and then write a biblical definition of faith.

3. What area(s) in your life do you find it difficult to apply what you believe and to exercise faith?

4. What makes *believing faith* difficult to practice?

It is one thing to believe in God; it is quite another to believe God.[15]

~ R.C. Sproul

The Shield Protects Us as We Take Shelter Behind It

The shield serves both as a protective barrier and a fire extinguisher. As we stay behind it, we are safe. In Genesis 15:1, when Abram was struggling with fear, God identifies Himself as a Shield to Abram, "…Do not fear, Abram, I am a shield to you; Your reward shall be very great." Later on, in Deuteronomy 33:29, He says that He is a Shield to Israel.

5. Read Deuteronomy 33:26-29 and record how God reveals Himself to you in this passage.

Our protection is God Himself. In Proverbs 18:10 Solomon writes, "The name of the Lord is a strong tower; The righteous runs into it and is safe." During the time Solomon lived, a person's name was not just what he was called. A name had a deeper meaning. It referred to the person's character. What Solomon is saying is that by His very character, God protects His righteous ones. The more we know of Him, the stronger we stand in the battle. The less we know of Him, the more likely we are to fall prey to Satan's fiery darts. Since God wants us to experience a deeper and more intimate knowledge of Himself, He allows the attacks of the enemy so that we will run to Him and experience His deliverance.

The more we know of Him, the stronger we stand in the battle. The less we know of Him, the more likely we are to fall prey to Satan's fiery darts.

The words "fiery darts" referred to an arrow with its tip wrapped with fabric and soaked in flammable fluids so it would burn with raging flames. Sometimes, these arrows were specially crafted, long, slender arrows that looked harmless on the outside, but inflicted severe, if not fatal damage, because the hollow interior of the arrow was filled with flammable fluids that, upon impact, exploded into violent fire.[16] As a protective measure, shields were repeatedly soaked in water throughout the battle to serve as fire extinguishers to quench the flaming onslaught.

Often when the devil strikes, his attack may seem negligible at first, like pesky little arrows that can do little damage. But when those arrows strike into our heart, they can cause a minor issue to develop into a fierce, flaming situation. The damage done in such a moment is very serious. But it could have all been avoided if our shield of faith had been held high and soaked in the Word of God.

The Shield Is Our Faith in the Word of God and the God of the Word

There is a sacred technique to being able to wield the shield of faith with expertise. And that is to be able to quote the Word of God and stand upon it.

6. Read Matthew 4:1-11. What verses did Jesus quote to overcome the destructive tactics of Satan when he was confronted in the wilderness?

If Satan would attack the Son of God, there is no doubt that he will try to shoot his arrows in your direction. But having a shield of faith saturated in the Word of God is dual protection against these attacks. It is a surety that the enemy's fiery darts will have little or no effect, even if they get close enough to strike your heart, mind, or emotions in the middle of whatever battle you find yourself facing today. And how many darts does Paul say the shield will extinguish? ALL. Not just those aimed at our minds. Not just those aimed at our hearts. Not just those aimed at our peace. The Shield of Faith is the one piece of armor that will protect us from absolutely all the darts…if we will utilize it every moment, every day.

Do you have victory verses for the battle? Write them out on index cards as a reminder of the overcoming power of God's Word. Memorize and meditate on those verses until you are so saturated in His truth that you will be able to quickly and deftly extinguish every dart Satan sends your way.

7. Can you remember a time when you were hit with a fiery dart that would have had destructive power, except that your shield of faith was Word-soaked, held high, and as a result, that attack had very little impact in your life? Take a moment to reflect and write about that situation.

To Take Up the Shield We Must Trust God

Paul makes it clear that action is required for us to wield our shield in spiritual warfare. We must take it up. What does that mean practically? Priscilla Shirer explains it well, "…faith is acting like God is telling the truth. The key thought here is action…It is the process of adapting your behavior, your decisions, and ultimately, your whole lifestyle so that it accords with what God has asked you to do—without needing to see the evidence that it will all work out in the end."[17]

Faith is an action verb. It is calling those things, which *are not* yet, as though they *are,* by our actions. Active faith in God and His Word is the shield of protection that will protect us against the attacks of the enemy. As David writes in Psalm 28:7, "The Lord is my strength and my shield; My heart trusts in Him, and I am helped; Therefore my heart exults, And with my song I shall thank Him."

A closing thought. For centuries, it was common for a soldier to carry his coat of arms on his shield. The coat of arms was a special design on the shield that was used as a symbol of their identity. As believers, our identity is deep-rooted in the cross, the place Jesus won the ultimate victory.

Spurgeon writes this beautiful description of the believer's coat of arms:

> …I think the Christian's best coat of arms is the cross of His Savior—the blood-red cross, always stained, but never stained, always dyed in blood, yet always resplendent with ruby brightness, always trodden on, yet always triumphant, always despised, yet always glorified, always attacked, yet without resistance, coming off more than conqueror.[18]

He continues with this challenge:

> Let that blood-red cross be your choice, then when your battle is over, they will hang your shield up in heaven, and when the old heraldries have gone, and the lions, and tigers, and beasts, and all manner of strange things have vanished from remembrance, that cross and your old shield indented with many a blow shall be honorable with many a triumph before the throne of God! Above all things, then, take the Shield of Faith![19]

In Christ, we have the victory! Amen and Amen!

A few months ago, I was walking down a flight of stairs in an antebellum house in Savannah, Georgia that had a low clearance. As I descended the staircase, there was a handwritten sign posted, "Watch your head." In other words, "Be careful or this staircase will take you out!"

The moment we stepped from spiritual darkness into the kingdom of light through faith in Jesus Christ, we enlisted as soldiers under the waving banner of the cross to battle against the powers of darkness until victory is won. And regardless of where your battle is being fought today, the admonition, "Watch your head" is a warning that must not be taken lightly. Head protection is vital in warfare because anything without a head is…well…dead.

The fifth piece of God's armor is designed to protect our heads from the assaults of Satan.

The Helmet of Salvation

Paul simply states, "take the helmet of salvation" (Ephesians 6:17a). What he is saying is, "Remember to protect your head."

Just before going into battle, the Roman soldier would put on a helmet. These helmets were either made of bronze or of leather with pieces of metal covering it. The helmet also usually had a chinstrap, a visor, and extended to cover the back and sides of his neck to provide as much protection as possible. What did his head need to be protected from? Certainly he needed his head safe from arrows that were flying around on the battlefield. But also from a lethal weapon known as a broadsword. You've seen this bludgeoning force in the movies. The broadsword was three to four feet long and it had a massive handle that was held with both hands like a baseball bat. In battle, the idea was that a soldier would lift it over his head and then deal a crushing blow to the brain of his opponent and basically, as John MacArthur says, "create split personalities."[20]

So girlfriend, watch your head! Just as our brain governs our physical body and tells it what to do, our minds control our spiritual being. Our minds are the battlegrounds of our lives and we must keep them protected from absorbing the blows of the enemy, that cruel liar and accuser.

Notice that I didn't write that we are kept from the blows of Satan, because he never sits out a round in the battle and is well aware of the damage he can do to our minds. But, we do not have to absorb the blows. And when our helmet of salvation is on, we won't.

Proverbs 23:7 is a warning for us to wear our protective head gear at all times, "For as he thinks within himself, so he is."

1. What are some of the ways the enemy attacks our minds?

When Satan bombards us with discouragement, doubt, despair, depression, defeat, distorted thoughts and a lot of other things that don't begin with the letter "d", any old helmet will not suffice. We must put on the helmet of salvation. Let's look at what might be a misconception about the helmet of salvation.

2. Read Ephesians 1:1,3. Who was Paul writing this letter to?

His Ephesian audience was already saved. With that being understood, the helmet of salvation does not refer to our initial salvation experience. Linguistically, when the suffix "ation" is added to a word it indicates an action or a process. The salvation Paul is writing about in reference to the helmet is the entire process of salvation, past, present, and future, as taught throughout Scripture. When we put on the helmet of salvation, we are to think about all of life from the perspective of God's full salvation.

The progression of our full salvation is a three-fold "ation" process:

- Justification. The removal of the penalty of sin, occurring at the time in the past we received our new life in Christ (Romans 3:23-24).

- Sanctification. This is our present tense salvation. It is the ongoing transformation of a believer into the image of Christ, the process by which we are delivered from the power of sin (James 1:21).

- Glorification. This is our future with Christ for all eternity when we are transported, once and for all, from the presence of sin (1 John 3:2-3).

Sanctification is the salvation that Paul is referring to with the helmet of salvation. It is the present tense process of becoming more like Christ. Are you becoming more like Christ—holy, loving, serving and giving—or are you being torn apart, drug down, beat up (and perhaps ready to give up!) by the onslaught of Satan and his demons?

3. Read Colossians 2:6. What are believers commanded to do?

Take a moment and consider your present, right now, today walk with Christ in light of the past work of salvation He accomplished on your behalf.

4. Read Romans 12:2. How is your transformation process going?

J.B. Phillips' paraphrase captures the meaning of Romans 12:2, "Don't let the world around you squeeze you into its own mold, but let God re-mold your minds from within, so that you may prove in practice that the plan of God for you is good, meets all His demands and moves towards the goal of true maturity." Paul is telling us that we are not to be conformed to this kind of thinking where God is not the center and circumference, the mindset that typifies people who have a shallow relationship with the eternal God. Instead, our focus should be on pleasing and glorifying Christ, keeping eternity on the forefront of our minds.

5. Read Isaiah 26:3, 1 Corinthians 14:20, and 1 Peter 1:13. What instruction do these verses give regarding the mind?

We cannot afford to leave our minds unprotected or the enemy will try to cripple us with lies, negative thoughts, and vain imaginations. If we allow thinking that is not intentionally and energetically focused on God and His will to take root in the soil of our hearts, eventually all of our thoughts and actions will adapt to the lies, keeping us from achieving the purpose for which we were created.

6. Read Colossians 3:2 and Philippians 4:8. Using these verses as a biblical basis, what would you tell someone who is struggling with wrong thought patterns?

> *If we allow thinking that is not intentionally and energetically focused on God and His will to take root in the soil of our hearts, eventually all of our thoughts and actions will adapt to the lies, keeping us from achieving the purpose for which we were created.*

When the enemy tries to bombard us with his libelous ways, we cannot allow his lies to take root in our hearts. We must actively and vigorously replace those lies with God's Truth because "the Word of the Lord is right and true" (Psalm 33:4, NIV).

Search God's Word for what He says is true about you. Start believing and memorizing those true statements about you. The following statements and verses will get you started:

- I am significant. (1 Corinthians 12:27)

- I am valuable. (1 Corinthians 7:23)

- I am forgiven. (1 John 1:9)

- I am treasured. (1 Peter 2:9)

- I am precious. (Proverbs 31:10, 1 Peter 3:4)

- I am capable. (Ephesians 2:10)

7. What are some additional statements and corresponding truths from the Word of God that apply to areas the enemy attacks you?

Make no mistake about it. A never-ending war is raging all around you. And yes, Satan and his demons are relentless and cruel. They may send every kind of debilitating thought imaginable our way, but with our helmet in place, we can fend off and defeat whatever attack he sends our day. And in the hope-filled words of the hymn, keep in mind:

> The strife will not be long;
> This day the noise of battle,
> The next the victor's song.
> To those who vanquish evil
> A crown of life shall be;
> They with the King of Glory
> Shall reign eternally.[21]

No Roman soldier would go to all of the trouble to put on each piece of his armor and then head to the battlefield, leaving his weapon behind. To do so would be the equivalent of battlefield suicide. While the five pieces of armor we have already examined provided protection from the attack of his foe, they could not kill the enemy. Only a sword could do that.

Without a sword, a soldier had no chance of survival if his enemy got close enough to engage in hand-to-hand combat. In ancient warfare, there were two types of swords. One was the massive broadsword that we looked at yesterday; the other, the *machaira*, was a shorter double-edged sword that ranged from six to eighteen inches in length. This smaller sword was used in battle with a solitary foe defensively to deflect incoming blows from an opponent and offensively to deliver a fatal strike. It was carried in a sheath or scabbard and was always at hand, ready to use.[22]

If Satan cannot take us out from a distance, he will move in for the close kill.

1. Read Ephesians 6:17. What instruction does Paul give for those times when we are face to face with the enemy of our souls?

The Sword of the Spirit

Paul explains that this sword comes from the Holy Spirit and then adds that it is the Word of God.

2. Read Hebrews 4:12. How does the writer describe the Word of God?

In Hebrews, the author uses the Greek word *logos*, which refers to the written Word. In Ephesians 6:17, Paul uses the Greek word *rhema*, the spoken Word which is the declaration of the written Word applied to a specific situation. In other words, the written Word is the basis for the specific sword thrusts of the spoken Word that defeat the enemy.[23]

We saw Jesus model this as he battled Satan in the wilderness in Matthew 4:1-11. Three times, in response to the enemy's attack, Jesus answered, "It is written" and then quoted the Word of God. Jesus knew what weapon to use. And what was best for Him is best for us. Spurgeon writes:

> "It is written." Stand upon it, and if the devil were fifty devils in one, he could not overcome you. On the other hand, if you leave "It is written," Satan knows more about reasoning than you do. He is far older, has studied mankind very thoroughly, and knows all our weak points. Therefore, the contest will be an unequal one. Do not argue with him but wave in his face the banner of God's Word. Satan cannot endure the infallible truth, for it is death to the falsehood of which he is the father.[24]

God's Word, this incredible, matchless, incomparable book, our weapon, is at our disposal at all times in the battle against Satan. But, as is true of all weapons, it has to be put into use. Paul tells us that we have to "take" our sword; action is required on our part for our weapon to be effective. To avoid falling victim to the enemy, we have to know exactly what God's Word is.

3. Read the following verses and record what you learn about God's Word.

	God's Word Is
Psalm 19:7	
Proverbs 30:5-6	
Revelation 22:18-19	
Isaiah 1:2	
Isaiah 55:11	
2 Peter 1:21	

Infallible. Inerrant. Complete. Authoritative. Sufficient. Effective. Divine. That is the weapon we have in the Word of God. The nineteenth century Scottish preacher, Thomas Guthrie summarizes,

> The Bible is an armory of heavenly weapons, a laboratory of infallible medicines, a mine of exhaustless wealth. It is a guidebook for every road, a chart for every sea, a medicine for every malady, and a balm for every wound. Rob us of our Bible and our sky has lost its sun.[25]

We must live in the Word and have the Word living in us or we will not be effective in the battle. Satan is wily and will find out where we are ignorant and attack us there. We have to know the Word of God if we expect to be victorious in the fight. The best method for getting God's Word into us so that we are properly equipped for warfare is one that I heard Adrian Rogers share many times:

Read it through.

Think it clear.

Write it down.

Pray it in.

Live it out.

Pass it on.[26]

Once we know God's Word, we must be prepared to use God's Word. It is not a weapon designed by human hands, but a weapon with a divine Source and Power.

4. Read John 14:17, 26. What do we learn in these verses about the Holy Spirit?

John MacArthur explains, "…the Holy Spirit is the believer's resident truth Teacher, who teaches all things and brings God's Word to our remembrance."[27] Our weapon is the sword of the Spirit, and He will not abandon us in the thick of the battle. Of that we can be sure.

Now, there is one more thing we need to know about our sword. It endures.

5. What did Jesus say in Luke 21:33?

The sword of the Spirit is our conquering weapon that equips us to go on the offensive against anything and everything the enemy brings against us. It is indestructible. We can count on it in every circumstance of every battle.

How do we stand firm in spiritual warfare? When Satan and his demons try to steal our peace and joy, rob us of sleep, snuff out our hope, eradicate our energy, dismantle our dreams, wreck our witness, nullify our efforts, crush our calling, and swallow up our lives, we STAND FIRM by putting on the full armor of God and going into battle with our sword swinging.

The armor is not for a museum where we go and look over its strength, but it is for the battlefield. Polished armor hanging up in the hall of our creed will not save us in the day of battle. . .You must come to Calvary for each piece of this wonderful armor. When we come and take it for ourselves, we can see that our whole body is covered. We are to 'be able to stand against' the enemy. Stand, Christian, in the victory Christ wrought on Calvary.[28]
~ Henrietta Mears

Entangled

How the Enemy Enslaves

The strongest chains are not those that can be placed around the body,
but those that are wrapped around the mind and heart.[1]
~ Ray Stedman

We must understand the adversary's schemes to be able to stand firm against them, fully surrendered to the Lord and suited up in the armor He has provided. When we are standing in all the fullness of Christ, we are able to prevail.

As we saw last week, the real battlefield is in our minds. The enemy is relentless in shooting fiery darts into our minds. It is as these thoughts take hold that we begin the downward spiral into the sin that they entice. Consequently, we must do battle to take control of our thoughts.

Neil Anderson and Timothy Warner write:

> Every action is just a product of our thoughts. 'For as a man thinks within himself, so he is' (Proverbs 23:7, NASB). The will can only act on what the mind knows. Wrong information, lack of knowledge, or a faulty belief system can lead to undesirable and even destructive actions…Life comes down to the principle that if we believe right we will live right, but we need to understand that right belief is more than right knowledge – people may not live what they profess, but they will always live what they believe.[2]

That is why to ignore spiritual warfare because it makes us feel uncomfortable or because it is not a popular topic will only be to our own demise. The enemy has always sought to have people either be over interested in spiritual warfare or to ignore it altogether. It is time for us to deal with those sins and strongholds that have enslaved us.

Read 2 Peter 2:18-22. Focus on verse 19, especially this phrase: "for by what a man is overcome, by this he is enslaved". We are enslaved in our minds. We act out of what we believe. That is why the enemy schemes against us with fiery darts aimed for the mind.

1. What wrong way(s) of thinking have you enslaved?

2. Read Proverbs 5:22-23. With what do these verses tell us we are held?

The word for cords in the Hebrew means, "cord, a rope, a line, something twisted, a snare"[3] or a noose. In other words, we hang ourselves with our own sin!

Look closely at 2 Peter 2:20-22. These verses do not describe an actual convert to Christianity, but one who has through knowledge of the Lord left their sinful lifestyle only to return back to it. It is only after we have been born of the Spirit that we are able to have victory over sin.

3. Describe a situation when you have seen someone return to his or her sin.

4. How do we ensure that as believers we do not become ensnared by sin?

5. Read Colossians 3:1-4. How do you keep your mind "set" on things above?

The Bible is very clear that our thoughts determine our actions and that what we have set the affections of our heart upon will drive our choices. Recently, I asked a friend of mine, Jenny Weaver, who happens to be a surgeon, to explain the way the brain works and how we can take thoughts captive and actually retrain our brains and thus our actions. The following was her response:

> The brain is an extraordinary organ, and not well understood. Here are a few fun facts we *do* know about the brain, but don't let these blow your mind (couldn't resist that one):
>
> • the human brain only weighs 3 pounds, but receives a whopping 30% of the blood circulation;
>
> • the old saying that "we only use 10% of our brain" is false: we actually use most of our brain, most of the time;
>
> • the brain has no pain receptors and cannot feel pain, which is why surgeons can operate on a person's brain while they are awake;
>
> • the brain can make new neurons, or brain cells, and incorporate them to make new neural pathways well into old age; this means *we can unlearn old ways of thinking and learn new ways of thinking,* essentially training our brains to think differently!

As someone "thinks within himself, so he is" (Proverbs 23:7).

Let's have a brief lesson on how the brain works, because this will help us understand how we "take captive every thought to make it obedient to Christ" (2 Corinthians 10:5). The brain contains many cells called neurons, which are the foundation cells of brain function. Neurons contain a cell body which processes signals between cells. From these cell bodies extrude finger-like extensions called dendrites, which receive signals from other neurons. Also attached to the cell body is the axon, which is like a long arm that reaches out to pass signals to other neurons. Nerve impulses are electrical signals that travel via the dendrites, cell body, and axon repeatedly from neuron to neuron across connections called synapses. These impulses can connect over thousands of neurons to produce functions such as memory, recall, muscular movements, and nearly everything in the body. When impulses travel down neurons in sequence, this is called a *neural pathway*.

These neural pathways are generally formed by repetition, and an old saying related to brain function is: "neurons that fire together, wire together." This basically means *the more that you do something, the more the neural pathway gets forged in your brain*. Repetition also causes the neurons involved in the pathway to become myelinated, which means they become covered in a fatty substance called myelin that insulates the nerve, and increases the already remarkable rate at which impulses are conducted. These myelinated pathways, because they are faster and insulated, then become the brain's default pathways, when thoughts or stimuli are encountered. Here's the good news about how God created our brains: they are highly plastic, which means *they can change*.

We have the ability to create new neural pathways, even generate new brain cells, no matter our age (per research from Columbia University, published 2018). These new neural pathways, in time and with usage, can then become our new default pathways when stimuli (such as other thoughts, behaviors, interactions) are encountered. So when we experience the flaming arrows of the enemy in our minds, or when we are plagued with our own destructive thought patterns, even those that have been reinforced over years by others around us, we have the God-given ability to change our brain response to those things, and make them submit to the power and authority of Christ. This isn't easy, and it isn't quick. It requires intentionality and prayer. But as it happens, our new neural pathways become our new thought patterns. And since our own thoughts and human reasoning are worthless compared to God's, we want our thoughts to be rooted in Scripture, which means we have to know Scripture. "My people are destroyed for lack of knowledge" (Hosea 4:6). How greatly would our lives be transformed if our "default neural pathways" are the Word of God!

"Whatever is noble, whatever is right, whatever is pure, whatever is lovely, whatever is admirable – if anything is excellent or praiseworthy – think about such things" (Philippians 4:8).

How do we make these new neural pathways? Repetition. Even more specifically, multiple cognitive studies have shown that *spaced repetition* is best for retention and retrieval. Spaced repetition is essentially the opposite of "cramming" – it means to review something you are trying to learn at multiple intervals of time, rather than repeating it multiple times at one sitting. For memorizing Scripture, this is why many people find it effective to keep a box of index cards, or a ring of cards, and review some verses daily, some weekly, and some at longer intervals.

There are several Bible memory apps that help you learn Scripture in multi-modal ways (quizzes, fill in the blank, games, etc), which have been shown to increase retention. These apps will also pull up verses at intervals to learn by spaced repetition. All of us struggle with certain negative thought patterns, or sinful behaviors, or ungodly reactions to things we regularly encounter. Those negative neural pathways may have been developed over many years, and maybe strongly ingrained in our brains. We can work daily to create new neural pathways to combat those thoughts with God's Word. For example, if I struggle with getting easily angry, or defaulting to fear-based living, or comparing myself to other women, then I can find verses that directly deals with these issues and memorize them. It takes intentional effort and repetition to then directly speak to these thoughts or temptations with these scriptures, but in time and with more repetition, these new pathways can develop and undergo greater myelination.

Another interesting fact that research has shown is that as we develop new pathways, the old pathways actually "prune" themselves, and decrease in myelination and synapses. So our old way of thinking can slowly decrease while our new way of thinking can slowly increase. And eventually we train our brains to default to the Word of God, which is our offensive weapon, the Sword of the Spirit.[4]

Read 2 Corinthians 10:3-5 again. This passage gives us a Biblical explanation of what Jenny just explained.

1. What does this passage tell us we are battling against?

2. How are speculations raised up against the knowledge of God?

The enemy will seek to fill our minds with speculations. I was listening to an author on Christian radio many years ago. She stated that we have five seconds to deal with a thought. She said if we don't deal with it, it will deal with us.

I have found this to be true in my own life. If I don't stop a wrong thought the moment it enters my consciousness, it will begin to take hold of my mind and then hijack my emotions. This is where the enemy has a heyday by mounting an assault of speculations. Then anxiety and worry take over and fear becomes almost impossible to overthrow.

Since this battle is not against a person, it is not your spouse, parent or co-worker who is at fault. It is the evil one behind their actions that have "pushed your buttons" and elicited the angry, impatient or fearful response.

I have found that I must stay alert and be ready for the fiery darts of the enemy. The following simple process has helped me take thoughts captive and learn to replace the lies of my flesh and the enemy with the truth of God. I have written out an example for you to see.

> **Recognize it** – Any fearful or anxious thought.
>
> **Refuse it** – The moment I sense an anxious thought, I refuse it entrance.
>
> **Resist it** – I resist the enemy and acknowledge that this thought originated with him.
>
> **Replace it** – Replace the lies of the enemy with God's truth. "God has not given us a spirit of fear, but of love, and power and a sound mind" (2 Timothy 1:7).

3. Take this simple process and work through one of the lies that the enemy uses to keep you in bondage to the flesh. Beside Recognize it, write down the lie. Then write down how you will Refuse it, Resist the evil one and then select a scripture that you will use to Replace the lie. Remember, we act out of what we believe!

Recognize it –

Refuse it –

Resist it –

Replace it –

Christians who aren't filling their minds with scripture are like warriors
going out to battle without a helmet.[5]
~ Chip Ingram

Chip Ingram writes these challenging words:

> Are you beginning to get an idea of how serious studying and meditating on Scripture and renewing your mind are? This is not a matter of squeezing in that brief, daily devotional with a chapter of Bible reading and then thinking, 'Okay, check. I've done that. No need to feel guilty now.' This is the substance of life. Psalm 119:105 says that God's Word is a lamp to our feet and a light to our path. Moses told the children of Israel that they were to take to heart every word he commanded them. For this word 'is your life' (Deuteronomy 32:47)…Over and over again we get a clear, biblical picture that God's Word is a life-and-death matter. Like a sword in the hand of a soldier, it needs to become second nature. [6]

If we truly believe that the Word of God "is our life," we will study it diligently and apply it to our lives. It is through the application of God's Word that we tear down strongholds and every speculation that is raised up against the truth (2 Corinthians 10:3-5).

Wrong ways of thinking that have erected a house of lies in our minds must have the structure weakened through the Sword of the Spirit and be brought down through the blood of Christ and His Word!

My first encounter with someone who was demonized was early in our ministry. At that time, I served in the youth department on Wednesday evenings, so I was not in the sanctuary the evening that Kelly (not her real name) and her husband entered after the service had started.

Wrong ways of thinking that have erected a house of lies in our minds must have the structure weakened through the Sword of the Spirit and be brought down through the blood of Christ and His Word!

My husband was preaching and noticed them slip into the back of the sanctuary. At the end of the service, as he extended the invitation for people to come to Christ, this couple came forward. Kelly told my husband that demonic spirits had tormented her for years. She told him that she heard voices and was at the end of her rope. She needed help!

My husband invited Kelly and her husband to join him in his office. She described a childhood of witchcraft and ritual abuse. Not having ever encountered anything like this, he called a very wise and godly prayer warrior and asked her if she would be willing to meet with Kelly and her husband. Mrs. Ellen (not her real name) agreed to ask her pastor to join them to pray with her and help her find freedom from the enemy.

Mrs. Ellen's pastor, who had experience on the mission field, agreed to meet with them if my husband and I joined them. He said that the Lord had brought them to our church and thus must want us to be involved.

We all met a few days later in the pastor's office. The pastor instructed us to pray while he prayed over Kelly and asked the Lord for wisdom and discernment of spirits. The Lord granted this pastor great wisdom and insight. He called out demonic spirits and brought the name of Christ and the blood of Jesus against the evil one. The enemy had been given entrance through her mother's witchcraft and the satanic ritual abuse she had encountered as a child. At the end of almost two hours of prayer, Kelly slumped over as though asleep. The pastor stepped back and said, "This may be the first real peace she has ever experienced".

As Kelly raised her head, she exclaimed, "The voices are gone!"

The pastor then instructed Mrs. Ellen to go home with Kelly and her husband and pray over their home. He told them if there was anything in the home that did not honor Christ to remove it, and if they found anything pertaining to witchcraft to burn it.

That sweet church embraced this couple and Mrs. Ellen met with and discipled Kelly in the Word of God and her new–found freedom. The pastor told us that her situation was one of the worst he had ever encountered. He said, the Lord must have wanted us to understand the tactics of the evil one and how to stand firm against his schemes and help others find freedom in Him.

I have never forgotten that encounter. I had always believed in the spirit realm. I had seen lives transformed through salvation and fully delivered from a life of sin. But I had never known anyone who was demonized and tormented like this young woman. The power of the Name of Jesus and His blood authoritatively applied by this pastor sent the devil fleeing.

1. Read Acts 19:11-20. The power of the Holy Spirit was evident in Paul's life and he took authority over demonic spirits. What happened when some Jewish exorcists tried to expel demonic spirits?

2. How did the demonic spirits respond?

3. What does verse 17 tell us was the result of this encounter?

4. What did the people who had books of magic and witchcraft do with these materials?

5. What do we learn from this encounter?

WEEK 7 · DAY FOUR

We have a choice. We are able, through the power of the Holy Spirit, to choose to set our minds on the things of the Spirit and the things that our Lord values. The enemy uses his tactics to divert our attention and affection away from the Lord. We must choose!

Let's take another look at some verses in Romans 8.

1. Read Romans 8:5-7. Notice the references to the mind and how we choose to think. What does this passage tell us about those who set their minds on the things of the flesh?

2. What is the result of the mind set on the Spirit?

Jerry Rankin explains,

> Our attitudes and actions are controlled by the volitional choices we make in our mind. The victory doesn't come automatically just because we are in Christ. The battle is in our mind and in our hearts. We are vulnerable because Satan speaks to our minds. He shapes our thoughts and perceptions, enticing us to be self-serving, to gratify carnal desires and embrace the values and things of the world. This was the way we lived by default before knowing Jesus Christ and being born of the Spirit.[7]

3. Read Romans 8:8. Based on this verse, who pleases God?

4. Read Romans 8:9-17. What is the proof that we are children of God?

This passage of Scripture tells us that we are fellow heirs with Christ. One of the ways we combat wrong ways of thinking is to focus on what we have received because we are "in Christ".

5. Make a list of what Christ purchased for you through His death, burial, and resurrection. To help you get started, go back to the first of the workbook and read the *Declarations of Who We are in Christ*.

If you say there's no hope, you're listening to the father of lies (John 8:44). You've encountered the thief who comes to steal, kill, and destroy (John 10:10) – the one who's determined to keep you a failure, to defeat you on every front he can. The only way you'll bring him down, the only way you'll extinguish those fiery arrows that will impale you on the stake of continuous defeat until you're consumed in its flames of destruction is through the Word. His Word is truth, and it alone can sanctify you – set you apart for victory. You may think there's no recovery from your failure. But my friend, if you have God, you have a future – and it's not a dismal one.[8]

~ Kay Arthur

Read 2 Peter 2:17-19 in the New Living Translation:

These people are as useless as dried-up springs or as mist blown away by the wind. They are doomed to blackest darkness. They brag about themselves with empty, foolish boasting. With an appeal to twisted sexual desires, they lure back into sin those who have barely escaped from a lifestyle of deception. They promise freedom, but they themselves are slaves of sin and corruption. For you are a slave to whatever controls you.

> *God never intended for you to just survive. Jesus Christ died to defeat the works of the evil one and to give you the power to live the Christian life to the fullest.*

God never intended for you to just survive. Jesus Christ died to defeat the works of the evil one and to give you the power to live the Christian life to the fullest. In her book, *Praying God's Word*, Beth Moore states why she thinks the concept of strongholds seems to be increasing in popularity: "I believe that the primary answer is the timing of our generation on God's kingdom calendar. The Word of God clearly teaches us that satanic activity and influence will increase dramatically as the day of Christ's return draws nearer. Revelation 12:12 says of Satan, 'He is filled with fury because he knows his time is short'."[9]

The enemy promises freedom and uses others to influence us to believe his lies because he knows if we compromise, we will become a slave to the sinful stronghold that controls us. Let's review what we have learned this week.

1. Review Day One. Are you choosing to "set your mind on things above"? How are you choosing to do this on a daily basis?

2. Review Day Two. How are you doing recognizing wrong thoughts?

Are you choosing to refuse, resist and replace them? Sometimes you must consciously refuse and resist. The more you do it, the easier it will become. If you are struggling with a certain sin or stronghold, share it with a trusted Christian friend or mentor and ask them to pray for you. The accountability is helpful, but sometimes, just speaking and confessing brings the sinful thought into the light and it loses its hold on you.

3. Review Day Three. How serious are you about walking blamelessly with our Lord and not giving the devil a foothold (Ephesians 4:27) or entrance through willful sin? What scriptural truth are you standing on to refute the lie that the enemy uses against you?

What area do you find most difficult to overcome?

Here is a list of some of the most common sinful strongholds:

- Unforgiveness and Bitterness
- Pride
- Sexual Bondage
- Rebellion
- Worldliness and Materialism
- Unbelief
- Addiction
- Negative or Critical Spirit
- Insecurity or Rejection

Add to the list anything the Lord reveals to you that has held you captive and prevented you from experiencing all that Christ purchased through His death, burial and resurrection–the abundant life!

We need to be equipped, and we begin by knowing God's Word and believing it enough to live it! Begin to apply God's Word to your life and stand on it. You will begin to experience a new level of freedom and power in the Holy Spirit as you appropriate God's Word and allow Him to renew your mind (Romans 12:2) and thus your actions.

So my first purpose is to alert you that there's a battle going on. My second purpose is to help equip you to fight the good fight of faith, to stand in the victory Christ has provided. You see, I don't ask people, 'Do you have the victory?' That's the wrong question. What we need to ask is, 'Are you standing in the victory you already have in Christ?'[10]

~ Jim Logan

Be on the Alert

Overcoming Prayer, Part 1

The first recorded attack of Satan was upon the family, and as the twentieth century comes to a close, Satan is still attacking the family. [1]
~ Jim Logan

The Family

As we have said many times, the devil tries nothing new under the sun. His schemes and tactics have been the same from the beginning. His sights are set on you, your marriage, your family and your children. He is no respecter of persons, age, position or power. He seeks to devour and destroy you and your family.

In his book, *Reclaiming Surrendered Ground*, Jim Logan says, "When one family member is being defeated by the enemy, it can have devastating effects upon the whole family."[2]

As my pastor often says, "A day without prayer is a wasted day." Reflect back on this morning. The alarm went off much earlier than you'd like. Your toasty feet emerged from the warm covers and met the chill of the morning. You stumbled to the coffee pot wiping your sleepy eyes. To whom or what did your thoughts go? Think about it.

Before we begin our day, speak a word to our family, engage in conversation, or tackle our to-do list, we must hear the call of our Savior, "Come and talk with Me…" (Psalm 27:8a, NLT). He longs to hear from you. He longs to speak to you. When we set aside time to meet with Him in prayer, we not only declare our need for Him, but also announce to the enemy that there is no place for him.

Let us set our minds on heavenly things as we strive to be on the alert through the power of prayer!

1. Write out Ephesians 6:18. How do we live this out in day-to-day life?

Sylvia Gunter rightly states, "Prayer is not a nice add-on, an optional extra. It is your life."[3]

2. Can you truly say that prayer is "your life?" If not, what stands in your way?

As we begin this week's study on prayer, I want to share a word of personal testimony. I have greatly benefited over the years as I've listened to how God has worked in the lives of other believers. Personal testimony cannot be disputed or denied. As I pen these words, I am asking God to use them in your life to call you to a fiery, devoted prayer life.

I was raised in church and in a Christian home, so prayer has always been a familiar concept. I've done it and I've heard it done thousands of times. But then, I *experienced* it. There is a difference. We can go through the motions of praying. We can listen to others pray. And we benefit from both of these. Through in-depth Bible study, discipleship, and having a pastor and his wife passionate about prayer, I began to really understand prayer. Intellectually, I understood that I could talk to God. But to grasp that I could boldly enter the throne room of heaven and lay my praise and petitions directly at the feet of Jesus took it to another level for me.

I began to make prayer a priority. I developed a method that worked for me and it has changed my life. The only wrong way to pray is to not pray at all.

Learning this came by way of some hard times in my life. I found myself desperately needing God, so I began calling out to Him. He showed me that He was all I had and He would become all I needed. I came to know Him in a way I'd never known Him. I began to hear Him speak to me like never before. I was convinced that He was waiting for me each morning, to both hear from me and to speak life into me. In fact, I sometimes wondered how He could be tending to the universe because I was convinced all His focus and attention were on me as I sat in my spot and talked with Him. His Father heart has a way of doing this for us. If you are not experiencing this, you can. He wills and desires that you do. You will never be the same.

I want to share with you how I pray each morning. As I've already said, there is not a right or wrong way to pray. Find a method that works for you and get after it! When I got serious about prayer, I bought a small box at a local craft store and filled it with index cards and tabs (pictured here).

As you can see, I have divided it into several categories...husband, children, family/marriage, extended family, others, me, city/nation and answers. Over the years, I have added cards as I've read in my daily quiet time, listened to sermons and lectures, talked with godly friends, etc.

Each morning, I begin my prayer time with praise by saying, "Let all that I am praise the LORD; with my whole heart, I will praise His holy name" (Psalm 103:1, NLT). Then I go through cards with attributes of God that He has revealed to me. Following my time of praise, I begin to go through my tabbed sections. I pull several cards from each section and pray through them. As I finish, I move those cards to the back of that section so I am continually rotating through the cards. When someone asks me to pray, I jot it down and make a card for it when I get home. This ensures I will not forget to pray! And one of my very favorite parts is recording the answer, along with the date, on the back of the card as God answers! What an encouragement to see Him answer specifically and then to periodically go back and remember all the ways He's been faithful. He does not always answer the way I'd hoped for, but He does always answer. Being reminded of His faithfulness is a boost to your faith and will keep you coming back for more!

3. As you think about developing a prayer method or continuing what you've started, read Psalm 102:18. Why might it be important to pray and keep a record of it?

Prayer is radically and gloriously encountering God, knowing
Him better and loving Him more. [4]
~ Sylvia Gunter

Be on the Alert

WEEK 8 · DAY TWO

We've all heard the phrase, "timing is everything." Today is no exception. As my fingers tap across the keyboard for today's study, I am overwhelmed at the timing of my Savior. This time it wasn't easy or blissful, but it is powerful. The circumstances of my week have been Father-filtered in order to equip me to write this lesson. God has used them so I can confidently stand and proclaim to you… THERE IS POWER IN PRAYER!

The last several days have been hard. Excruciatingly hard. My husband and I recently made a commitment to pray together each night before bed (answered prayer). Wouldn't you assume that only good would come from such a wonderful idea? From the moment my husband uttered the words, the devil has set his sights on me, my children, and our family. That is how he works. I've heard it said that we should be such a threat to the kingdom of darkness that when our feet hit the floor in the morning, the devil shrieks, "Oh no! She's up!" And when we pray, he is certainly threatened.

So before we dig in this week on how we can pray for our families, let us first honestly evaluate our individual prayer life.

In his book, *Pray Like It Matters*, Dr. Steve Gaines says, "No one ever prayed like Jesus. When it comes to prayer, He truly is 'the expert.'"[5] He has given us the blueprint on prayer, by example and throughout His Word.

1. Read the following verses. What do these verses teach us about prayer?

    Mark 1:35

    Luke 5:16

WEEK 8 | 169

Psalm 5:3

Psalm 143:8

Robert Velarde gives a beautiful definition of prayer. He says, "Prayer is a relationship, wherein we humbly communicate, worship, and sincerely seek God's face, knowing that He hears us, loves us and will respond."[6]

Do you begin each day by communicating with Him, worshipping Him and seeking His face? God hears you. God loves you. And God will respond to you. It is His nature, the very essence of His being.

Our perspective is often skewed. We see only what lies right in front of us. God has a perspective far beyond anything we can imagine. He was and is and always will be. There is nothing He hasn't seen, doesn't see, and will not see. Jim Logan says, "He knows what's happening at every point along the way. That's why I need His wisdom. I can't act on my perspective alone. Wisdom is the ability to see life as God sees it."[7]

To see life as God sees it. This is life changing! James 1:5 tells us that we simply have to ask for wisdom and God will give it. We can do this as we meet with Him in prayer and be confident that He will give generously! Then, we are able to walk through our days with HIS perspective rather than ours. A pure heart will open our eyes to see God (Matthew 5:8). This comes through prayer as we confess our sin and profess our needs for THIS day (Matthew 6:11).

I recently read an article that described our prayers as arrows. The author said we should be "skilled archers in the discipline of prayer, with prayers like arrows."[8]

Hopefully, you are in the habit of praying Scripture. This is a sure way to pray God's will for your life and others. If not, use these verses to begin this practice.

Ps 143:5
Prov. 3:5
2 Tim 1:7
Is 46:4

2. How can you use these verses to pray for yourself?

Exodus 33:18

Psalm 119:37

Psalm 86:17

Psalm 119:33

John 15:5

3. Are there other scriptures you pray regularly for yourself? Consider sharing these with your small group. (As other women share, write the references down so you can use these as you pray.)

As I opened this day by sharing a recent struggle, I want to remind you that as soon as you commit to begin each day in prayer and pray God's Word over your life, you are placing a bull's-eye on your back. The enemy will be that much more determined to derail you. He will begin firing his darts of temptation, discouragement, fear, anxiety and hopelessness at you and those closest to you. Jim Logan writes, "Being on the winning team doesn't mean you are excused from the battle."[9] Quite the contrary...being on the winning team puts you on the front lines of the battle.

> *When you pray, you unleash resurrection power over yourself and over those you bring to the throne room of Heaven.*

BUT...WE DO NOT HAVE TO FEAR! We do not live as those without hope (1 Thessalonians 4:13). As Logan says, "Jesus dealt the knockout blow at Calvary. He disarmed the demonic world."[10]

Dear sister in Christ, get on your knees. The victory has been won! Satan is a defeated foe and Jesus Christ is alive and reigns forevermore. He battled on the cross and won. The same power that raised Him from the dead lives in you, child of God! When you pray, you unleash resurrection power over yourself and over those you bring to the throne room of Heaven.

It starts in you. It starts in me. Will you commit right now to follow Jesus' example of praying each morning before you do anything else? Will you commit right now to see the world from God's perspective rather than yours? Will you commit right now to pray God's Word over yourself and recklessly abandon yourself to the perfect will of God?

Standing firm in these last days calls for a woman who is committed to specific and fervent prayers. Will you purposefully and passionately shoot your arrows of prayer to the throne room of Almighty God?

It is not the arithmetic of our prayers — how many they be;
nor the rhetoric of our prayers — how eloquent they be;
nor their geometry — how long they be;
nor their music — how sweet their voice may be;
nor their logic — how argumentative they be;
nor yet their method — how orderly they be;
nor even their divinity — how good their doctrine may be, which God cares for:
but it is the fervency of spirit which availeth much.[11]
~ Bishop Joseph Hall, 1808

WEEK 8 · DAY THREE

Are you married? Are you engaged? Do you hope to be married? Do you have a married friend? Do you have a son, son-in-law, grandson, or brother?

My guess is most everyone can answer "yes" to at least one of these questions. There is most likely a man in your life in some capacity that fills (or will one day fill) the role of husband. We, as women, like to remind everyone of all the responsibility we bear...and we do bear a lot of responsibility. However, we can easily forget the call on the men in our lives.

So regardless of your place in life, please do not check out on today's study. Dig in and allow the Lord to speak to you about praying for your husband (or someone in your family who is a husband).

From the beginning, God clearly defined the role of a man. The Bible goes on to specifically guide men in the role of husband. Obeying Scripture in this area points others to the gospel of Jesus Christ. Think of the weightiness that comes with being a godly husband.

1. What are some responsibilities of a husband?

    1 Corinthians 11:3

    Ephesians 5:25

    1 Timothy 5:8

Sylvia Gunter says, "Because you are one flesh with him, no one else stands in as strong a position in your prayers for him as you do. Make your husband your daily prayer priority."[12]

Do not be vulnerable or ignorant of the devil's schemes. Perhaps you're thinking, "My husband is one of the godliest men I've ever known. He walks closely with the Lord and I have nothing to worry about." Oh, dear friend, you just enlarged the target on your husband and marriage. Praise God, if this is your story. You have much to be thankful for and should treasure the fact that your husband is a devoted Christ follower. However, you would be falling prey to the tactics of the evil one if you believe your husband and marriage are immune to falling short of the glory of God.

In case you haven't noticed, men are very different from women. Shocking news, right? We naturally share our concerns and burdens with our girlfriends. We take comfort and find encouragement as we talk about life's struggles with a friend. Men do not typically do this. They usually internalize their deepest fears and weaknesses. It is incumbent upon us to stand in the gap and wage war against the devil on their behalf. We can do this most effectively through prayer. As one author writes, "Satan desires to destroy your husband, especially his character and his leadership in your relationship. Trust God through prayer as you daily surrender your husband and marriage to the Lord's wise, loving care."[13]

2. I want to use today's study to share some of what God has laid on my heart over the years to pray for my husband. Take your time in looking up these verses and record the things you can pray specifically for your husband. I also encourage you to write one of the verses out from time to time and let him know how you are praying for him specifically.

Psalm 1:1-3

Job 1:1

Psalm 19:13-14

Ephesians 1:17

Matthew 6:13

Psalm 101:3

James 4:7-8, 10

Romans 13:14

Ephesians 4:29

1 Thessalonians 5:17

2 Timothy 2:22

This diagram and scriptures are another tool you can use to pray for your husband:

PRAYING FOR YOUR HUSBAND
FROM HEAD TO TOE

Pray for His Brain:
Ask that God would keep it sharp and focused and that his thoughts would not be conformed to this world, but would be transformed and renewed by the power of God. (Romans 12:2)

Pray for His Eyes:
Ask that he would guard them diligently and would set no worthless thing before them. (Psalm 101:3)

Pray for His Ears:
Ask that they'd be tuned to hear God's still, small voice and that your husband would always remain attentive to the Holy Spirit's promptings. (1 Thessalonians 5:19; Isaiah 30:9)

Pray for His Mouth:
Ask that no unwholesome talk would proceed from it, but only what is good for building others up. Pray that your husband would always and only speak the truth in love. (Ephesians 4:15, 29)

Pray for His Heart:
Ask that Christ would sit enthroned upon it, that your husband would love God with all his heart and soul and might, that he'd love his neighbor as himself. (Mark 12:30-31) Pray for his heart to remain soft toward you (Proverbs 5:18-19), and to be knitted to the hearts of his children. (Malachi 4:6)

Pray for His Arms:
Ask that God would strengthen them and make them firm. Pray that your husband would take delight in his labor and that God would bless the work of his hands. (Psalm 90:17, Ecclesiastes 3:22)

Pray for His Legs:
Ask that God would give him strength and stamina, that your husband might run with endurance the race that is set before him, without growing weary or fainting along the way (Hebrews 12:1; Isaiah 40:31)

Pray for His Feet:
Ask that they'd be quick to flee from temptation, to turn away from evil, and to faithfully pursue wisdom, righteousness, peace, love, and truth. (2 Timothy 2:22; Psalm 34:14; Proverbs 4:5-7)

http://lovinglifeathome.com

14

Using the Word of God, pray for him from the top of his head to the soles of his feet.
Present every part of his body to God. [15]

~ Sylvia Gunter

"You'll never be a perfect parent, but you can be a praying parent. There is nothing you can do that will have a higher return on investment. In fact, the dividends are eternal."[16]

~ Mark Batterson

Dear sisters, please do not skip past today's study if you do not have children. Undoubtedly, there are children in your life that come to mind immediately.

Stormie Omartian says, "We can be a friend, a teacher, a grandparent, an aunt, a cousin, a neighbor, a guardian, or even a stranger with a heart of compassion or concern for a child. If you're aware of a child who doesn't have a praying parent, you can step into the gap right now and answer that need. You can effect a change in the life of any child you care about."[17]

Whatever your role in the life of a child, you can commit to storm the throne room of Heaven on his or her behalf. While there is nothing new under the sun, our children face decisions and struggles today that look differently than those we encountered. Technology is just one of the ways the world and the devil stays in the faces of our children, seeking to destroy their lives.

The sobering news in parenting is that we cannot ultimately choose Christ for our children. We have no control over their free will as they contemplate the narrow gate versus the wide gate. As Mark Batterson writes, "You can't choose Christ for your kids, but you can pray that they choose Christ."[18]

1a.   Read Isaiah 55:10-11. What does this verse teach about the power of God's Word?

1b.   As a parent, how does this encourage you as you share the truth of God's Word with your children and pray it over them?

As a mom, I sometimes think my role is to make sure my children believe every biblical truth I've shared with them. My job is to share it. God's job is to accomplish what He desires and to achieve His purpose for them.

We must come to God with open hands, offering our children to Him. After all, they belong to Him anyway. How can we expect God to move in their lives if we're parenting with a clutched fist? Release is hard. Letting go and relinquishing control is one of the most difficult aspects of parenting. However, as we release, we are exemplifying our faith and trust in the One who created them, knows them best, and loves them more than we do.

2.   What are some things that prevent you from releasing your children?

3.   Read Matthew 7:11. Why can we trust God with our children?

Step out of the way so God can accomplish His will for their lives and give them His best. Allow Him to use you as part of His work. "Be a special utensil for honorable use...ready for the Master to use you for every good work" (2 Timothy 2:21, NLT).

When my babies were born, I determined to be a praying parent. I have not done this perfectly, but I have done it consistently. I do not say this boastfully, but out of a heart that has desperately needed the Lord as I've been raising warriors for Christ. About five years ago, the Lord laid on my heart to take this to another level. I'd always prayed for my boys, but He was calling me to more. I have come to know the power of prayer experientially. It is my lifeline. I am convinced that I cannot raise these children for the glory of God without a significant amount of time on my knees. I am also convinced that my boys need a praying mom. One who will wake early on their behalf. One who will plead for their hearts as they venture out into the world apart from me. One who will pray them through their weaknesses and strongholds. One who will plead with the Lord to tear down and destroy every banner the enemy has raised up against them. It is my duty and privilege to stand...and kneel...on their behalf.

Tony Evans says, "Satan and his demons will try everything they can to stop you from praying because prayer is the tool through which the armor of God manifests its greatest potential for victory."[19] Satan knows the power of prayer. And he knows the power of prayer on behalf of our children. I believe his greatest tactics are doubt and discouragement. Do you ever doubt that God will do what you're praying for? Do you grow tired and weary from praying the same things for your children? Cling to the truth from the book of James which says, "The earnest prayer of a righteous person has great power and produces wonderful results" (James 5:16b, NLT).

Pray consistently. Pray boldly. Pray fervently. Pray continually. I encourage you to pray through your children's strengths and weaknesses. No one knows these aspects of your children like you do. Lay these out before the Lord and ask Him to shape and use them in your child's life.

Here are some ways I pray for my children. I do these almost every day.

- As I fold their laundry, I pray for their bodies. I pray for physical and spiritual protection over each and every part.

- When I finish my quiet time in the morning, I pass by their rooms. I extend my hands into their rooms and bathrooms and ask the Lord to unleash His Spirit. I ask Him to make Himself known to them as they open God's Word and begin their day. I ask that the enemy be bound from the moment they set their feet on the floor.

- I pray for each child before they get out of the car at school. Even when we've had a bad morning (and I feel more like pushing them out), I pray them out, asking for God's protection over them. I pray that they will carefully determine what pleases the Lord as they go throughout their day.

- As we pray in the evenings, I pray a blessing over them. (I often pray this same blessing as they leave to go to school or other events.) I lay my hands on them and say, "The Lord bless you and keep you; the Lord make his face shine on you and be gracious to you; the Lord turn his face toward you and give you peace" (Numbers 6:24-26). Find a blessing to pray over your children regularly.

4. What are some ways you pray for your children (or grandchildren)? Consider sharing with your small group.

I have a prayer box full of cards that I pray for my boys. I want to leave you today with some of my favorites. Look up these verses and add them to your arsenal. Consider sharing with your children the ways you are praying for them. This will encourage their hearts (even the teenage ones!).

5.   What can you pray for your children according to these scriptures?

Luke 2:52

1 Timothy 4:12

Colossians 1:9-10

Jeremiah 32:39

1 John 5:21

2 Samuel 22:22-24

Deuteronomy 13:4

2 Timothy 2:22

Psalm 42:1

Ephesians 5:10

Make sure the Heavenly Father hears about your kids daily! [20]
~ Mark Batterson

When you have suited up for battle in the heavenlies,
prayer is your ticket to take you straight into the heart of it. [21]
~ Tony Evans

This week's study has focused on praying for our families and ourselves. As we prepare for spiritual warfare and become more equipped to deal with our enemy, the devil, I pray the Lord has confirmed in your heart the urgency in praying over your family.

This morning as I was driving home after school drop-off, the Lord laid a specific need on my heart to pray for one of my children. I did not feel like praying because it was the same prayer that seemed to be on repeat. I told the Lord as I began, "God, I'm tired of this. I'm weary from praying the same thing over and over again. It seems like nothing is happening and it feels pointless to keep saying the same words time and time again." By the way, the Lord can handle your honesty. He's a big enough God to hear your raw frustration and disappointment. Laying your heart out before Him in those desperate moments is an aspect of prayer that only draws you closer to Him. He knows your heart anyway. He knows every word you're going to speak before you speak it. Watch your intimacy with Him deepen as you open up the deepest parts of your soul in prayer.

As I uttered these words and headed home to write for today, God spoke to me from James 4:8 saying, "Come near to Me and I will come near to you." He was encouraging me (and you) to keep coming to Him. As I do, He comes to me. Jim Logan says, "So at the very time when you feel most inclined to pull away from God, He urges you to draw close. If you will do that, what will He do? He'll draw close to you." [22] Do you see Satan's tactic here? He knows the Word of God and the power of God. He will do all he can to make sure you do not draw near to God because he knows the other side of the equation.

Me drawing near to God + God drawing near to me = Intimacy, Power, Victory

Revisit the account of the fall of Jericho in Joshua 6:1-27. Here we see God's miraculous power as a result of obedience. As we saw in week two, the people of Israel had just crossed into the land of Canaan. After wandering for forty difficult years, their challenge was to take the land of Canaan, the Promised Land. The first obstacle was the walled city of Jericho. God gave them specific instructions to march around the city seven times. Can you imagine the thoughts running through their minds? They had to think this was senseless, hopeless, and irrational. Perhaps they uttered words similar to my prayer this morning. Yet, Joshua followed God's instructions to the letter. And as a result, what seemed an insurmountable obstacle came crashing down.

1. Read Romans 15:4. Why were these accounts recorded in the Old Testament? What do we gain as we recount them?

The account from Joshua should teach us to trust God's way rather than the way of man. We cannot fully understand prayer, yet God calls us to pray throughout Scripture. We cannot fully understand God's timing, yet He's proven that it is always perfect. We cannot fully understand God's purposes, but His Word assures us that they are "plans to prosper you and not to harm you, plans to give you hope and a future" (Jeremiah 29:11b, NIV).

The walls of Jericho collapsed by the supernatural power of God. This same power is available to us today. When we march around our walled cities in prayer, we can do so with faith in a God of unswerving promises.

When we march around our walled cities in prayer, we can do so with faith in a God of unswerving promises.

John Piper says, "Isn't it significant that in the Bible...we don't have the statement 'You pray too much or too long'? We don't have a statement that says, 'You have things I did not want to give you because you kept on asking me when it was time to quit.' We don't have anything like that."[23]

2. What do these verses teach us about prayer?

James 4:2

Luke 18:1

Matthew 7:7

In her book, *Fervent*, Priscilla Shirer says, "All of our marriages and families are a big deal . . . because each one is a billboard for the eternal, unchangeable love story between God and humankind. Each of their successes or failures is of great importance, both in God's eyes and, therefore, in our enemy's eyes."[24] Your family matters. You are a walking billboard for the kingdom. What an incredible opportunity we have to share the gospel with a lost world! As we seek to point others to Jesus Christ, we must intentionally and passionately pray for our family. This equips us to stand firm in these last days and to wage war against the devil and his demons.

When you commit to pray God's Word over your family, you are summoning "the will of God down from heaven to earth and are a dangerous threat to Satan."[25] Your family is worth it. The time you spend in the presence of God on the behalf of your family is worth every second. Time in prayer is never wasted time. There is not anything better you could be doing for your family. I want to encourage you today. Do not grow weary. Keep on praying.

Maybe you are seeing God answer prayers and move mountains. Keep praying. Perhaps you can relate to my prayer this morning as you continue to whisper the same words. Keep praying.

3. Read Psalm 25:14. What do we learn about those who fear the Lord?

I believe part of fearing the Lord (a sense of awe and respect) is entrusting Him with our prayers and approaching Him with confidence (Hebrews 4:16). As we fear Him, He confides in us. We can be so close to Him that He shares the secret things with us. To know the secrets of the Lord, to experience His revelation, is an invaluable benefit for those who walk closely with Him in prayer.

4. One of my favorite verses to pray over my family is Hosea 4:6. How can you pray this verse over your family?

A lack of knowledge of the Scriptures and a rejection of that knowledge is dangerous for your family. Pray against this. The enemy strives to keep you from knowing the truth. His methods feature deceit and lies. No matter the condition of your family and its relationships, commit to fervently pray. No one, no family is immune to the attacks of the enemy. If you are a family who professes the name of Jesus Christ, it is the intent of the devil to destroy you from the inside out.

In addition to praying *for* your family, I encourage you to pray *with* your family. The Lord desires unity for His children. The devil seeks to divide. One of the surest ways to fight the attacks of the enemy on your family is to be a united front. Focuses on the Family authors write about praying together:

> In addition to strengthening each individual's connection with God, prayer has the side effect of deepening interpersonal relationships. It encourages family members to become more sensitive to one another's feelings. Prayer is all about *intimacy*– with the Lord and with one another. The familiar, time-worn saying is true: *families who pray together stay together*. That's because shared experiences of prayer quickly become opportunities to express mutual love, forgiveness, and grace. It's hard to hold on to grudges and cherish resentments when we're on our knees together before the Lord. As an act of shared intimacy, prayer creates family cohesiveness and strengthens the bonds between husband and wife, brother and sister, parent and child.[26]

Prayer is earthly permission for heavenly interference.[27]
~ Tony Evans

WEEK 9

Be on the Alert

Overcoming Prayer, Part 2

The Church and the World (Government Leaders and the Nations)

To pray for the church, we need to make sure we are in a right relationship with the Lord so we can stand in the gap on behalf of our local congregation and the church universal. The church is impacted by the sins of the members who make up the local body of Christ. Quite often, these sins that the Bible calls the Sins of the Fathers are so familiar that we don't even recognize them. Because we were most likely raised in a family where these sins were a part of the family dynamic, they have become our "normal".

Jim Logan provides a biblical context for the "sins of the fathers." Read his words from *Reclaiming Surrendered Ground*:

> The first occurrence of this concept (sins of the fathers) is in Exodus 20:5, in the giving of the Ten Commandments. After forbidding Israel to make or bow down to any "graven image" God tells Moses, "I the Lord thy God am a jealous God, visiting the iniquity of the fathers upon the children into the third and fourth generation of them that hate me."
>
> If this were the only time God said this, it would be no less important. But the same warning occurs at least four more times in the books of Moses: Exodus 34:7; Leviticus 26:39-40; Numbers 14:18; and Deuteronomy 5:9. In addition, the prophets refer to the concept of iniquity's, or sin's consequences upon children in Isaiah 14:21 and Jeremiah 14:20.
>
> The reference in Leviticus 26 is very interesting. God is warning the people of Israel that if they are unfaithful to Him, He will bring punishment on them and drive them from the land. But if the people confess their iniquities and the iniquities of their fathers (v. 4), He will remember His covenant promises to previous generations and restore them (v. 42).

In other words, the blessings of righteousness and faithfulness to God pass on through generations. Why should it seem strange that the consequences of sin and rebellion against Him would do the same in modern times?[1]

Sinful strongholds tend to get progressively worse from generation to generation. The sins we don't deal with will deal with us and they may destroy our children!

Be on the Alert

WEEK 9 · DAY ONE

When we think about our own families and the sinful patterns that have impacted us, it is not difficult to discern how the enemy works. Remember, his goal is to steal, kill and destroy (John 10:10). Sometimes it is easier to see these patterns in others. Let's take a look at Abraham, the man God called to be a blessing to the nations, and his descendants.

1a. Read Genesis 12:10-20. What did Abraham do when he and Sarah were traveling to the Promised Land and they encountered a famine?

1b. What did he ask Sarah to do to protect him?

God is sovereign. His plan will be accomplished. When God promised Abraham that he would have an heir whose descendants would outnumber the stars, He did not need Abraham's help to make this happen.

2. Read Genesis 16:1-2. What happened when Sarah intervened?

Abraham and Sarah had Isaac, the son of the promise. Isaac followed in his father's footsteps.

3. Read Genesis 26:6-11. What caused Isaac to lie?

4. Isaac and Rebekah were both deceivers. Read Genesis 27 and describe how the deception divided and brought great pain and separation to their family.

Think back to Sarah and her decision to "help" God out by offering Hagar to her husband. God had told Isaac and Rebekah when the twins were born that the older would serve the younger (Genesis 25:23). God did not need her help, but He did desire her obedience and cooperation.

5. How might things have been different if both women had trusted the Word of the Lord?

6. Read Genesis 27:13. What did Rebekah say to Jacob?

Did you know that these words would be fulfilled? When Jacob returned after being away for 20 years, his ailing father was still living, but his mother had evidently died because she was never mentioned again. The curse or "wages" of sin is death. The curse had come upon her, and she had experienced what she "said".

7. Where else have you seen this in Scripture?

The deceiver would be deceived. Do you see how the lying and deception is being passed down through the generations and goes on to wreak havoc? We will see as we continue to examine their families that the deception will ultimately lead to a desire to murder, which is covered up by more lies and deception.

It is interesting how baggage (sin) attracts baggage. The deceiver would not only be deceived but would marry a deceiver as well.

1. Read Genesis 29:21-30. How did Laban deceive Jacob?

2. Read Genesis 31:17-35. How did Rachel deceive her father?

Jacob's sons would later deceive Jacob when they sold Joseph into Egyptian slavery.

3a. Read Genesis 37. How did the deception divide the brothers and bring pain to their family?

3b. Looking at the circumstantial evidence (the coat with blood), Jacob believed his son had died. What was his response?

Putting circumstantial evidence over the truth of God leads to despair and disillusionment. Believing the truth leads to freedom.

4. When have you believed the lie of the evil one and fallen victim to fear and despair?

5. Make a timeline of events from Abraham to Joseph listing the lies and the results. Do you see the progression of sin and its effect?

Because of the cross, we have the power and authority to break any curse or sin pattern passed down through our lineage.

The good news is that Joseph broke the sin pattern that had been passed down through his family. Because of the cross, we have the power and authority to break any curse or sin pattern passed down through our lineage. Joseph, who had been betrayed by his own family and sold into slavery, honored Potiphar, his master. After being falsely accused by Potiphar's wife and thrown into prison, he did not give in to bitterness, but prospered there as well (Genesis 39-40). He refused to lie, or to satisfy his own sinful desires. He honored God and God was able to entrust him with great power and the deliverance of His people.

6. What is it that enables some people to handle power well and others to be crushed by it?

We are responsible for our own sin and rebellion. We can choose to love the Lord more than ourselves and sin will lose its hold. Could this be the very reason that Jesus said the greatest commandment was to, "love the Lord with all of your heart, and with all your soul, and with all your mind and with all your strength" (Mark 12:30)? This is an all-consuming love. God knows it is for our good and His glory, because through loving Him, sin loses. Which means love wins!

Ask the Lord to show you any sinful patterns in your family and take them to the Lord in prayer. The first step to victory over any sin is recognizing it. Then, just as we studied in Week 7, we must refuse it, and resist the evil one by replacing the lie, that we cannot overcome, with the truth of God's Word. Ask the Lord to give you specific verses to pray for yourself and your family.

Here is a great verse to obey and pray:

But the lovingkindness of the Lord is from everlasting to everlasting on those who fear Him, and His righteousness to children's children, to those who keep His covenant and remember His precepts to do them.
Psalm 103:17-18

Pray for Your Church

The Church of the Lord Jesus Christ is made up of redeemed humanity. We are all one family, baptized into Christ. Although we are all one family, we have local congregations that meet together just as the early church did in New Testament times. The local church is God's instrument to take the gospel to the nations and to care for its members.

Jesus told His disciples that people would know they belonged to Him by their love for one another (John 13:35). If we really love each other, we will stand with each other and pray for each other.

Paul was a leader, chosen by God to take the gospel to the Gentiles. He planted churches in every city he visited. These churches were very dear to him and he prayed diligently for them. There are several prayers in Paul's letters that are beneficial for us to pray as well.

1. Read Ephesians 1:15-19. Make a list of the specific things that Paul prayed for the Ephesians.

One of the best ways to learn to pray is to pray with someone who has an intimate walk with Christ. Paul knew Christ intimately and we can learn from his prayers.

2. Read Ephesians 3:14-21. List the things Paul prayed for them in these verses.

Notice how Paul moves into a doxology as he closes. Take a few moments to reflect on verses 20-21. Do you hear the confidence with which he prays? He knows to whom he is addressing his petitions and has no doubt that God is able and that He will answer.

3. How would you rate your level of faith when you pray?

As one author writes,

> In the battles of life, your peace is actually a weapon. Indeed, your confidence declares that you are not falling for the lies of the devil. You see, the first step toward having spiritual authority over the adversary is having peace in spite of our circumstances, When Jesus confronted the devil, He did not confront Satan with His emotions or in fear. Knowing that the devil was a liar, He simply refused to be influenced by any other voice than God's. His peace overwhelmed Satan, His authority then shattered the lie, which sent demons fleeing.[2]

We studied Ephesians 6 and the importance of appropriating the whole armor of God in Weeks 5 and 6.

Read Ephesians 6:18-20.

In these verses, we are made aware of the importance of suiting up for battle. The battle is fought in the spirit realm through prayer. Paul does not ask for release from prison, but for boldness to speak the gospel, as he ought to speak.

4. What do you think you would be praying about if you were in prison for your faith?

The church is the Bride of Christ. We are to value her and protect her (Ephesians 5:25-27). We are never to demean her. God has gifted us and called us to build up the church through our giftings that we might carry out the Great Commission.

5. What is your primary spiritual gift (1 Corinthians 12:1-11) and how are you using it in the church?

6. Write out a prayer for your church using some of the scriptures you studied today in Ephesians.

Pray for Your City

In 2007, the Lord led our staff and leadership to begin to pray diligently for our city. It was during this time that *Bellevue Loves Memphis* was birthed based on Jeremiah 29:7 which states, "Seek the welfare of the city, where I have sent you into exile, and pray to the Lord on its behalf; for in its welfare you will have welfare."

As we pray for the city God has called us to, we need to be strategic and specific.

The Bible is clear that righteous leaders are a blessing to a city and its people. Psalm 15 is a wonderful Psalm to pray for government leaders.

1. Make a list of specific things you can pray for leaders from this Psalm.

(You can access the names and profiles of political leaders in your city and in our nation online. I would encourage you to pray for them by name.)

2. Reflect on your city and its needs. Make a list of the strongholds the enemy has erected. These will be specific areas of sin that your city seems to be "known" for.

3. Now make a list of the Names of God that you can begin to pray over your city. Begin to bless your city to break the enemy's strongholds. Choose specific Names of God and Bible verses to refute the hold of the enemy.

Pray about ways that you can begin to make a difference in your city. As followers of Christ we are to be salt and light.

4. How are you taking the light of the gospel into your city and dispelling the darkness?

5. Make a list of churches in your city for which you will pray. Ask the Lord to bless and anoint their pastors and to protect them from the enemy and from compromising His Word. Pray that they will stand firm and be oaks of righteousness (Isaiah 61:3) for His Name's sake.

Spend time now praying for your city and for the churches in your city. Close your prayer time by praying a scriptural blessing over your city.

Pray for Your Country

We are commanded by God's Word to pray for our government leaders. Throughout God's Word, we are given examples of people praying for their cities and nations. In his book, *Onward: Engaging the Culture without Losing the Gospel*, Russell Moore writes,

> The church now has the opportunity to witness in a culture that often does not even pretend to share our 'values'. That is not a tragedy since we were never given a mission to promote 'values' in the first place, but to speak instead of sin and of righteousness and judgment, of Christ and his Kingdom. [3]

While we are to pray for the salvation of the citizens in our nation and take the gospel into a broken and hurting culture, it is not to save an American way of life, but to prepare people for the Kingdom of God. We will never "fit in" on this earth. When you become a citizen of Heaven, you realize that you are simply a pilgrim passing through. This world is not your home. Consequently, you are able to focus on fulfilling Christ's mandate as we journey toward our true home.

Our end goal is not a Christianized political party, but that God's Kingdom would come and His will would be "done on earth as it is in Heaven" (Matthew 6:10). The good news of the gospel is for all the nations.

While we are to pray for the salvation of the citizens in our nation and take the gospel into a broken and hurting culture, it is not to save an American way of life, but to prepare people for the Kingdom of God.

1. Read Daniel 9:1-23. What attributes does Daniel ascribe to God?

2. Look closely at Daniel 9:3. What methods did Daniel use to pray and how might you implement them?

3. What does Daniel repent of for his people?

4. Daniel was a righteous man who was told by Gabriel that he was "highly esteemed" (v. 23). What did Gabriel tell him was issued when he began to pray?

5. Following Daniel's example, how should we acknowledge God and His sovereignty in our prayers?

6. What sins should we repent of for America?

Here are some specific things to pray for America from Sylvia Gunter's book, *Prayer Portions:*

- Pray for an awakened church – John 17
  - A spirit of humility, repentance, and revival – 2 Chronicles 7:14
  - For the church to move in unity, love, and the power of the Spirit – John 17:23-24, 26

- Pray for pastors and Christian leaders who are God-anointed, God-appointed, and God-empowered and for a mighty movement of intercessory prayer that is aggressive in spiritual warfare.
  - God's protection and will – John 17:4, 11, 13, 15, 17, 19
  - For use of spiritual weapons – 2 Corinthians 10:3-4

- Pray for political leaders to repent, receive salvation and govern righteously, and for the "most unlikely" unrighteous people to be converted and become radical disciples. Pray for Christians in leadership to know their God and stand strong in the fear of the Lord.
  - Pray for all in authority – 1 Timothy 2:1-4
  - For just men (and women) to rule in the fear of the Lord – 2 Samuel 23:3

- Pray for the Lord of the harvest to reap multitudes for spiritual awakening and salvation and that new believers will be strong, growing disciples in the Lord.
  - God is not willing for any to perish – 2 Peter 3:9
  - That God's provision for sin be applied to the need of all those who do not know the Savior – John 17:25
  - That children and youth hear the gospel and learn the character of God and go forth as the "sent ones" – Mark 10:14-15[4]

The most effective way to live in victory over the devil
is to walk in righteousness with God.[5]
~Beth Moore

The Last Days
The Promise of His Coming

The bottom line is this: Jesus is coming, and I am certain of that and very glad. I have resigned from the program committee and have moved over to the welcoming committee. Even so, come Lord Jesus! [1]
~Adrian Rogers

My first exposure to the study of Eschatology—Last Things—commenced with the arrival of a new pastor at my church. Dr. Adrian Rogers arrived at Bellevue Baptist Church in the fall of 1972. It is difficult to describe the atmosphere as he began to preach the Word of God in those early days. Electric is the first adjective that comes to mind. I could not wait to get to church to hear the Word proclaimed. I longed to know it. "Like newborn babies, long for the pure milk of the word, so that by it you may grow in respect to salvation" (1 Peter 2:2). So, when Dr. Rogers began to teach on the Last Days and the Second Coming, a topic that I knew little about, I jumped right into the study and discovered it to be both amazing and complicated, yet one that every Christian should be acquainted with. It is a key doctrine of the Church. So, whether you are a novice or a seasoned student in the area of Eschatology, let's turn our attention this week to the Last Days.

Just as I came to consider Dr. Rogers as my spiritual father, the recipients of 2 Peter looked to the Apostle Peter for wisdom. As Peter transitions to a new topic at the beginning of chapter 3, he addresses the believers with the Greek word, *agapetos*, which may be translated as beloved, dear friends, dearly loved ones. His affection and concern for them as a spiritual father was evident as he outlined his concerns and issued a reminder and a warning. While our situations are vastly different from those believers, Satan's tactics remain amazingly similar—to create doubt concerning God's trustworthiness. We must be on guard.

The words of Peter are no less applicable to us as they were to the first century believers to whom he wrote. Warren Wiersbe appropriately reminds us: "How important it is for us as Christians to understand God's truth! Today we are surrounded by scoffers, people who refuse to take the Bible seriously when it speaks about Christ's return and the certainty of judgment."[2] As we look at "The Promise of His Coming," we will discover vital truth applicable for our day.

Read 2 Peter 3:1-9.

1. What admonition does the Apostle Peter give believers in verses 1-2?

2. What do the following representative verses reveal about what the believers should remember from the words of the prophets, the Lord Jesus, and the apostles?

   Isaiah 13:6-9

   Matthew 24:29-30

   1 Thessalonians 5:2-3

3. Relate the warning that Peter shares in 2 Peter 3:3-4.

Warren Wiersbe identifies scoffers or mockers in this manner: "A scoffer is someone who treats lightly that which ought to be taken seriously."[3] Then he continues: "Why do these apostates scoff? Because they want to continue living in their sins."[4]

4. What argument did the scoffers use to deny the coming of Jesus?

5. How does Peter refute the argument used by the scoffers and what does he bring to light that God had done in the past in verses 5-6?

Peter brings into focus the power of the Word of God. He speaks, and miraculous things happen— the creation, the flood. And there is another event on God's calendar, though we do not know when it will transpire.

6. What event does Peter mention in verse 7 and through what means is it accomplished?

Our all-powerful God undoubtedly can intervene in the affairs of men. He has in the past, and He certainly will in the future. He is not impotent, disinterested, or unable to change the course of nature. In the key verses of 8-9, Peter gently begins to unfold the very nature of God to the believers to explain why Christ's coming is right on schedule.

7. What does Peter disclose about God in verses 8-9?

The *Women's Evangelical Commentary, New Testament* sums up those verses beautifully:

> The seeming delay in Christ's return is not due to His indifference but rather reveals His patience and mercy. Peter was not teaching universalism—that God will save all mankind. He was simply stating that God desires that all will be saved, while knowing that many will reject Him.[5]

Not wishing for any to perish but for all to come to repentance.
2 Peter 3:9b

What a Savior!

Yesterday we began our study of eschatology as we considered the first nine verses of the third chapter of 2 Peter. Peter emphatically warns the believers about the scoffers who claimed that Jesus would not be coming back as He had promised, insinuating that He either could not intervene in the course of nature or was uninterested in returning. Peter corrects that misinformation by explaining God's perspective of time and His patience for all to come to salvation. Nevertheless, Jesus' second coming is on God's timetable. The Old Testament prophets proclaimed it and the Lord Jesus promised it. Today we will delve into this fathomless topic. We will only be able to give it a cursory look since countless volumes have been written about it.

1. What does Jesus promise in John 14:1-3 and to whom is it pledged?

2. Relate what the prophet Zechariah forecasted in Zechariah 14:1, 3-5.

3. What did the Holy Spirit convey to the Apostle Paul regarding the Lord's return in

    1 Thessalonians 4:16?

While these verses appear to be describing the same event, they actually refer to two facets of His coming—the Rapture of the Saints and Christ's Second Coming to judge the world. The prophets viewed the event from a distance, but on close observation of the Scripture, it appears to be actually two occurrences.

Dr. David Jeremiah clarifies it this way:

> From their time-distanced vantage point, the prophets saw the two peaks of the Second Coming as one mountain. They identified it as the second coming of Christ *with* His saints, but they failed to see there was another mountain—the second coming of Christ *for* His saints—separated from the more distant mountain by the valley of the Tribulation.[6]

This viewpoint correlates with the Pre-Tribulation view of the Rapture which holds that Jesus removes the church before the Tribulation. This is the perspective taken by our pastor, Dr. Steve Gaines, and our former pastor, Dr. Adrian Rogers, and the approach we will take in this study.

Though many passages of Scripture relate to the three topics we will consider—the Rapture, the Tribulation, and the Second Coming—let's contemplate just a few.

4. Read these two passages concerning the Rapture and record what you discover.

    1 Thessalonians 4:13-18

    1 Corinthians 15:51-52

5. Christ's Olivet Discourse found in Matthew 24 contains much insight into the End of the Age including the Tribulation and His Second Coming. Document the details.

In the midst of the Tribulation, the Antichrist and the minions of Satan are revealed, and the forces of darkness rage. But, we are reminded in the Word who wins this war. It began in a garden and has commenced through the centuries. The culmination is recorded in the book of Revelation.

6. What is documented in Revelation 19:11-21 regarding the last battle?

I am sure our quick trek through the Last Days left you breathless with a lot of unresolved questions. This study is a weighty and complicated one. In my studies, I found a summary written by Warren Wiersbe that I feel will be helpful to you—future events in a nutshell. It's a little long, but hopefully you can use it for future reference.

> Scholars of prophecy do not agree on all the details of future events. But the following summary is a fair representation of what many prophetic scholars believe as to the order of events:
>
> 1. The Rapture of the church (1 Corinthians 15:51-58; 1 Thessalonians 4:13-18). This can occur at any time.
>
> 2. The leader of the ten European nations makes a seven-year agreement with Israel (Daniel 9:26-27).
>
> 3. After three-and-one-half years, he breaks the agreement (Daniel 9:27).
>
> 4. He moves to Jerusalem and sets up his image in the temple (2 Thessalonians 2:3-4; Revelation 13).
>
> 5. The Antichrist begins to control the world and forces all people to worship and obey him. At this time God sends great tribulation upon the earth (Matthew 24:21).
>
> 6. The nations gather at Armageddon to fight the Antichrist and Israel, but see the sign of Christ's coming and unite to fight Him (Zechariah 12; Revelation 13:13-14; 19:11ff).
>
> 7. Jesus returns to the earth, defeats His enemies, is received by the Jews, and establishes His kingdom on earth (Revelation 19:11ff; Zechariah 12:7-13:1). He will reign on earth for 1,000 years (Revelation 20:1-5). [7]

> *The Lord's return is imminent—other things may happen before He comes, but nothing must happen before He comes.*

Quite frankly, as I was attempting to write this lesson, I was really struggling—so much material to cover and so little space. The enemy was certainly challenging my confidence. I got up from my computer and walked around while I mulled it all over. Then I decided a cup of coffee might help. (And I might have added a piece of left-over Halloween candy.) When I reached into the cabinet, I brought out a mug with "In Christ!" emblazoned across it. I hugged it to my chest and thought, "That's all I need."

All I need for anything. All I need to be ready for Christ's return. The Lord's return is imminent—other things *may* happen before He comes, but nothing *must* happen before He comes. Are you ready for the shout?

Throughout history, there have been times when the world seemed very dark and fraught with trouble—before the flood, during the times of the judges, in times of war and captivity, during the infancy of the church, in the corruption of the church before the Reformation, and even today, if we are honest. As Dr. Adrian Rogers said:

> The child of God does not have to walk around with 'headline hysteria.' Instead of becoming frightened and panicked when it looks like the world is coming apart at the seams, Christians can turn to each other and say, 'It's getting gloriously dark!'[8]

The battle between light and dark, good and evil, began in the Garden of Eden and continues until this day. As we saw in Week 3, Satan's strategy remains much the same as it was when he confronted Eve.

1. Read Genesis 3:1-6. What line of reasoning did Satan use in his temptation of Eve?

Dr. David Jeremiah delivers the following warning:

> Listen, the devil doesn't want to help anyone! He wants to destroy, not build. He wants to enslave, not liberate. Remember, he "walks about like a roaring lion, seeking whom he may devour." Of course, he never does it in an obvious or obnoxious way. He does it deceptively, by sowing little seeds of doubt about the Word of God.[9]

No doubt, as Peter penned his second letter to the believers refuting the scoffers, he was reminded when the enemy used fear to sow a seed of doubt in his mind, and he had done the unthinkable—denied His Savior.

Read Luke 22:31-34.

2. What do you discover about the ploy of Satan, Jesus' intervention on Peter's behalf, and His instructions for Peter? (We read this passage in Week 5, but you may want to review as you formulate your answer.)

From our perspective, we might have labeled Peter a washed-up failure, but not our Lord. He was forgiven and went on to be a mighty evangelist in the early church. As we see in the book of Acts, Peter followed the Lord's admonition as he and the other apostles stood fearlessly for the truth.

3. Review these passages from Acts and record the response of Peter and the apostles to persecution.

   Acts 4:18-22

   Acts 5:17-32

4. How do you think the church today is standing up to the attacks on God's Word?

A number of years ago, I received some audio tapes of a conference at a well-known seminary. As I began to listen to them, I was alarmed at what was being taught. Adam and Eve were referred to as a myth. The miracles did not happen. I couldn't believe my ears. It was my first exposure to liberal theology and the undermining of Scripture. This is one of Satan's greatest ruses. As mankind questions the veracity of Scripture, God's message to the world is challenged by unbelief, and Satan has accomplished his purpose. The attack on God's Word is a significant problem facing the church today. Dr. Jeremiah comments on this issue:

> In the name of "tolerance," today's church believes it must call God both "he" and "she" and that it must describe the mother of Jesus as a "young woman" rather than as the Virgin Mary. In the name of Christianity, groups such as the Jesus Seminar attack some of the faith's most sacred doctrines. According to the scholars of the Jesus Seminar, Jesus never claimed to be the Messiah. He did not predict the end of the world. The Lord's Prayer was drawn up by Christians after Jesus died and most of the Gospels tell us nothing of the real Jesus. And on and on it goes. Little by little, seductively, Satan sows his demonic seeds of deception and evil.[10]

If the church presents a watered-down Jesus, how in the world will a dying humanity be drawn to Him?

A wonderful testimony from the time of the Reformation highlights the great value one English priest placed on the Bible. Corruption had seeped into the church before Martin Luther nailed his 95 theses upon the church door and proclaimed that salvation was by faith alone. Because the Bible was written in Latin rather than the language of the people, Biblical ignorance was rampant even among the priests. But one brilliant priest, who could speak seven languages and was highly proficient in Greek and Hebrew, longed to translate the Scripture into English so that his countrymen would have access to God's truth and could read for themselves the doctrines of the faith. His name was William Tyndale. His dilemma was that it was against the law to translate the Bible into English.

Tyndale moved to Europe to begin his translation after failing to gain permission to translate from the bishop. He moved from city to city while the king's agents searched for him. He completed his translation and had it printed. But a fellow Englishman betrayed him, and he was arrested, thrown in prison, and convicted of heresy. On October 6, 1536, Tyndale was strangled and then burned at the stake. He was given an opportunity to recant, but he refused. How important was access to the Bible to him? He was willing to die for it.

5. William Tyndale was willing to die so that you could have access to the Bible in English. How would you evaluate your commitment to know the truth in its pages? Ask the Lord for insight.

6. Turn these verses into a prayer—Psalm 119:127-130.

In these days when our culture maligns God's Word, may we as Christians stand firm for truth.

It's getting gloriously dark!

Over the last century, the culture in the United States has dramatically changed. As Dr. Adrian Rogers used to say, "Sin that used to slink down back alleys, now struts down Main Street." Gradually, as philosophical thought has separated itself from the teaching of the church, mankind no longer feels it must answer to God. And things that were formerly only whispered about now have become mainstream thought and practice which are rolling through our society with a snowball effect. Dr. David Jeremiah comments on the effects of the resulting secularism:

> The unifying belief, which laid the foundation for the philosophy of secularism, is this: God, if He exists, is irrelevant. Humanity is calling the shots, and humans are evolving biologically, socially, governmentally, and morally. Forget about answering to a holy Creator. We are responsible for ourselves, and we can now govern our morality by societal consensus.[11]

The believer has become persona non grata in the battle for cultural influence in government, on college campuses, with moral issues, etc. Yet, we should not be surprised by any of this—grieved but not surprised—for we were warned in God's Word. It is a part of the struggle between good and evil, and we must be careful not to fall victim to its sway.

1. Read 2 Timothy 3:1-6 and 2 Timothy 4:3-4. Record what you learn concerning the last days and identify any characteristics that you see in culture today.

In his book *What In The World Is Going On?* David Jeremiah gives us an enlightening observation:

> In 1947, forward-looking sociologist Dr. Carle Zimmerman wrote a text called *Family and Civilization*. He identified eleven "symptoms of final decay" observable in the fall of both the Greek and Roman civilizations. See how many characterize our society:

- No-fault divorce
- "Birth Dearth"; increased disrespect for parenthood and parents
- Meaningless marriage rites/ceremonies
- Defamation of past national heroes
- Acceptance of alternative marriage forms
- Widespread attitudes of feminism, narcissism, hedonism
- Propagation of antifamily sentiment
- Acceptance of most forms of adultery
- Rebellious children
- Increased juvenile delinquency
- Common acceptance of all forms of sexual perversion[12]

What amazing insight!

2. From your perspective, what do you consider the five most crucial issues facing our culture today?

I posed the above question to my son, who is an ethics professor. He replied, "Gender, Sexuality, Marriage, Justice, and Poverty. You know, just small things. Nothing controversial." I smiled, but there is nothing humorous about these issues. Contentious debate surrounds them.

3. How do you determine your beliefs about divisive issues?

4. Are your decisions regarding the issues ever based on feelings or emotions?

Recently, I was speaking to the Bellevue Bookstore manager, Rick Jones, a passionate scholar in Apologetics, about the process of making wise decisions regarding the issues of the day. He insightfully commented, "If my emotions are driving my decisions, doctrine will always suffer." We should keep a tender heart toward the sinner, but take a strong stand against sin.

5. List the sins revealed in Romans 1:18-32 and God's response to mankind's rebellion against Him.

6. What admonition do you find in Colossians 2:8?

Under the banner of fairness, many philosophies are vying for our approval. All must be filtered through the Truth. When we disagree, there may be consequences. Increasingly, groups are challenging Christians who disagree with them. Dr. David Jeremiah outlines the stages of Christian persecution now appearing in our culture:

1. Stereotyping
2. Marginalizing
3. Threatening
4. Intimidating
5. Litigating[13]

Let's hold fast to truth regardless of the cost. We will close our study today with some encouraging words from Dr. Del Tackett with Focus on the Family:

> If we don't really believe the truth of God and live it, then our witness will be confusing and misleading. Most of us go through life not recognizing that our personal worldviews have been deeply affected by the world.
>
> However, by diligently learning, applying and trusting God's truths in every area of our lives...we can begin to develop a deep comprehensive faith that will stand against the unrelenting tide of our culture's nonbiblical ideas. If we capture and embrace more of God's worldview and trust it with unwavering faith, then we begin to make the right decisions and form the appropriate responses to questions on abortion, same-sex marriage, cloning, stem-cell research and even media choices. Because, in the end, it is our decisions and actions that reveal what we really believe.[14]

In 2016, my husband and I accompanied a group from three Southern Baptist seminaries on a study tour to England. I had long desired to go to England, but the opportunity to visit the historical Christian sites made it extra-special. Before I embarked on the trip, I was informed that England is a spiritually dark and secular country. Churches have been transformed into hostels and restaurants—others remain empty on Sundays. Yet, England has a rich spiritual heritage. During the Reformation, numerous Protestants gave their lives to provide Biblical truth to the masses. I visited Newgate Prison where Thomas Helwys, the first Baptist pastor in England, was imprisoned and probably died. I stood before a monument in Smithfield Market in London where Protestant martyr, John Rogers, was burned at the stake. Numerous times, I passed the beautiful Victorian memorial to the Oxford Martyrs Nicholas Ridley, Hugh Latimer, and Thomas Cramer, who were burned at the stake. Satan desires to silence us through persecution. But these martyrs speak on.

1. What insight do you gain on persecution from 2 Timothy 3:12?

2. Relate Paul's perspective on difficult times from 2 Corinthians 4:7-10.

3. What are the results of tribulation recorded in Romans 5:3-5?

Dr. David Jeremiah sheds some light on the persecution of believers:

> Many believe that worldwide persecution of Christians today is worse than at any time in history. Each month, 322 Christians are killed for their faith, 214 church buildings and Christian properties are destroyed, and 772 forms of violence are committed against individual Christians or Christian groups. Those figures add up to more than fifteen thousand incidents of serious persecution of Christians per year.
>
> Given the history and present state of Christian persecution world-wide, it becomes less surprising that we are beginning to feel the sting of it in the United States. To have a nation established on and aligned with Christian principles has been the exception historically. That alignment is now breaking down, and we are reverting to the historical norm.[15]

Is it getting gloriously dark in our country? If so, what are we to do? I have noticed that during difficult, dark days Christians tend to withdraw from the culture. And, indeed, as the culture becomes increasingly hostile, it is tempting. The choice is to escape or to engage. What will it be? Satan would bombard us with a million reasons to resist God's prompting. A man named Ananias from the book of Acts had a similar choice. Let's see what decision he made.

4. Read Acts 9:10-18. What assignment did God give Ananias and how did he respond?

5. How do you respond to God when He asks you to step out of your comfort zone?

Reflect on this account from Adrian Rogers about Joseph Tson from his book, *Kingdom Authority*:

> My Romanian friend, Joseph Tson, was being harassed by the Communist thugs in Romania. This was the time under the brutal dictatorship of Ceausescu. He was warned, "Joseph, if you don't get in line and register with the Communist government and let us control your ministry, you know what we can do to you." Joseph answered, "I know what you can do. Your chief weapon is killing, but let me tell you what my

chief weapon is. My chief weapon is dying. And I want to warn you, if you use yours, I will be forced to use mine."

When Joseph was asked what he meant by using dying as a weapon he said, "If you kill me, you will sprinkle every book I have written, every sermon that I have preached, with my blood. People will know that I believed enough in what I preach to die for it. So, if you use your weapon, I will be forced to use mine."

The Communist enforcer shook his head and went away bewildered.[16]

6. Will you choose to escape or to engage our culture? Spend some time in prayer as you consider this question.

Christians may not have the overwhelming influence we once had on the culture, but we can reach one—even the one that seems unlikely. I would like to share two examples from my trip to England. One day as we were visiting the memorial to the Oxford martyrs, one of the professors sat down beside a homeless man and asked him, "Do you know who these men were that this monument was erected for?" The man began to curse him and left. A day or so later, the professor spotted the man again, and the Holy Spirit prompted him to engage the man in conversation once more. He was reluctant but obedient. He bought the homeless man lunch and began an on-going conversation with him. And a homeless man in a hard situation in a dark country was gloriously saved.

We live in a spiritually dark country as well. So, switch your attention to the DFW airport where our group was waiting to board the plane for England. I noticed a woman on the periphery of the group listening intently to our conversation. I assumed she was a part of the group. Suddenly she asked, "How do you get started with this Jesus thing?" Immediately my son and some of the students began to share with her the way to salvation, and her life was changed forever. Interestingly, my son has a friend who is a pastor in the town where she lives, and he was able to connect the two. Coincidence? I think not—all a part of God's plan.

> *We have nothing to fear if persecution comes our way in these dark days. We have a Savior who keeps His promises.*

We have nothing to fear if persecution comes our way in these dark days. We have a Savior who keeps His promises. Let's engage our world till He comes.

Rejoice, the One whose name is Truth is coming for us. Even so come quickly, Lord Jesus!

The Day of the Lord
The Final Word

People do not become holy by wishful thinking. There must be study, consideration, deliberation, and sincere inquiry, or the way of truth will be missed. The commands of God must be set before us like the target to aim at, the model to work by, and the road to walk in.[1]
~ Charles Spurgeon

The Day of the Lord

WEEK 11 · DAY ONE

My husband and I were privileged to travel to Nigeria to teach pastors and church leaders about evangelism, discipleship, and church planting. Our busy teaching schedule left little time for much else. However, on the last afternoon of our stay our interpreter offered to take us sightseeing. I asked to visit the market. I wanted to buy a length of the beautiful fabrics used to make Nigerian garments for a keepsake. He knew a shopkeeper who carried textiles and was pleased to take us.

The market was bustling with people. The increased traffic noises and incessant horn honking announced we were in the near vicinity. Tiny metal cubicles lined the main street containing businesses of every description. Barbers, herbalists, furniture craftsmen, coffin makers, and peddlers vied for customers. Food was cooking over open fires. Fresh bread was randomly piled in handmade baskets. The fragrant smell of citrus indicated the location of various fruit vendors. Live chickens clucked from their woven basket coops. Goats, tied together with rope leashes, bleated and pawed at the ground. Open meat markets suspended sides of beef and pork from hooks in the ceiling. The butcher, in a dirty apron, carved the carcasses into abstract shapes. Women swept the dusty sidewalks and rearranged their wares. Several shopkeepers called to the passing crowds, hoping to entice potential customers to stop and shop.

Our translator parked in front of his friend's shop. As we slid out of the car, the shopkeepers pegged us as tourists and potential customers. The shop was barely more than a ten-by-ten-foot room. Several owners shared the tiny space. Neatly folded yard goods were stacked from the floor to the ceiling and crammed in every available space. The brilliant colors of the African fabrics created a life-sized kaleidoscope. In the middle of the shop, seamstresses sat at treadle sewing machines. Their feet peddled wildly, sending the needles skittering across the fabric as they created Nigerian fashions. The hum of the machines added to the chaotic background noise of the marketplace.

Immediately, the owners began to pull samples of their wares as they shouted animated greetings in their native language. They surrounded me with samplings of their selections, fanning out the colorful cotton fabric like the tail of a peacock. Despite the language barrier, each man was attempting to impress me with the merits of his product. A young boy rushed towards me with a small wooden stool in tow. He presented it with great flourish and indicated I was to sit down. Fabric was piled on my lap and stacked on the floor, encircling my tiny throne! All the while the shopkeepers were trying to seal their deal. The Nigerians give new meaning to customer service!

I pulled out a beautiful green fabric accented with a black paisley design and indicated I had made my selection. Our interpreter stepped up and dismissed all the potential sellers with a wave of his hand, except the man who owned the piece I wanted. The disappointed shopkeepers nodded knowingly and bowed low before stepping away from the ensuing negotiations. This was my first experience with haggling. Our translator and the shop owner squared off. We could not understand the words, but the body language was unmistakable. With raised voices, each man barked out his acceptable price while the other shook his head and stared at his opponent with disbelief and disdain. Back and forth the negotiating went. Our friend gestured wildly, indicating the price was outrageous, especially for guests to their country. In response, the shopkeeper made a gesture like he was being strangled. The volume escalated as I wondered at the wisdom of my purchase. Suddenly a deal was struck. A wide smile spread across the face of the shopkeeper as a rich chuckle came from our friend. Both men shook hands, affectionately slapping each other on the back. What just happened? As a bystander, I had the impression a knife fight was about to break out over my piece of fabric. In reality, haggling is a part of Nigerian culture. The shopkeeper bowed deeply as he presented my purchase to me. My husband paid the agreed upon price, which amounted to a couple of American dollars, and we thanked the shopkeeper for the fabric and the new experience!

In similar fashion, many Christians enjoy haggling over the details of eschatology (the study of prophecies of the last days). Passionate about their position, they are willing to argue the fine points of the Second Coming of Christ and the sequence of the following events. In truth, we cannot empathetically know the details of the last days. Much of God's revelation concerning this time is veiled in figurative language. This much we are certain of – Jesus will return for His people and God will judge the ungodly. As Peter writes, "The day of the Lord will come like a thief, in which the heavens will pass away with a roar and the elements will be destroyed with intense heat, and the earth and its works will be burned up" (2 Peter 3:10).

John MacArthur explains, "In Scripture the day of the Lord signifies the extraordinary, miraculous interventions of God in human history for the purpose of judgment, culminating in His final judgment of the wicked on earth and the destruction of the present universe."[2]

Be ready. Stand firm. The day of the Lord will come! MacArthur continues, "One day—in the relatively near future—this universe will be utterly destroyed. Under the weight of God's consuming wrath, in final retribution, it will melt away in a final holocaust of unimaginable intensity."[3]

Read 2 Peter 3:10-18.

When the Lord does come, it will be both surprising, like a thief, and catastrophic. The heavens will be eradicated. The earth will be obliterated. Peter challenges, "Since all these things are to be destroyed in this way, what sort of people ought you to be in holy conduct and godliness" (2 Peter 3:11). In light of his revelation of the coming destruction of the universe, a divine obligation rests upon the readers. Knowing of this truth, how should we live?

1. Paul gave an ample description of what the Christian life should look like, especially in light of the day of the Lord. Read 1 Thessalonians 5:12-23. Write the characteristics of a godly lifestyle. Put a star beside those spiritual disciplines you need to increase.

As we navigate our earthly sojourn, we should be heavenly-minded people. Unlike those outside a personal relationship with Christ, "we look not at things which are seen, but at the things which are not seen; for the things which are seen are temporal, but the things which are not seen are eternal" (2 Corinthians 4:18).

We are called to be "ambassadors for Christ" (2 Corinthians 5:20) to display the character and glory of our God. As we pursue godliness, good works will be the supernatural result. "For we are His workmanship, created in Christ Jesus for good works, which God prepared beforehand so that we would walk in them" (Ephesians 2:10). However, the Christian life cannot be reduced to adhering to outward behavior fueled by willpower. Rather, it is to be the manifestation of the life of Christ in us through the power of the Holy Spirit. This requires our entire soul–mind, will, and emotion – to be yielded to the Holy Spirit of God. Our mind must be renewed through the personal study of God's Word. Our will must be surrendered to the Holy Spirit by a predetermined decision to obey God's instructions. And our emotions, which tend to be fickle and self-protecting, must be allied with the will of the Father.

In an effort to fortify the sagging spirits of the persecuted church, Peter repeatedly reminds his readers to look back to the first coming of Jesus and His redemptive work on the cross and to look forward to the Second Coming of Christ.

As Matthew Henry explains,

> The first coming of our Lord Jesus Christ, when he *appeared in the form of a servant,* was what the people of God earnestly waited and looked for: that coming was for *the consolation of Israel,* Luke 2:25. How much more should they wait with expectation and earnestness for his second coming, which will be the day of their complete redemption, and of his most glorious manifestation! [4]

Remember beloved, we are citizens of Heaven. This world is not our home; we are "aliens and strangers" (1 Peter 2:11). Like Abraham of old, "we are looking for the city which has foundations, whose architect and builder is God" (Hebrews 11:10). "According to His promise we are looking for new heavens and a new earth, in which righteousness dwells (2 Peter 3:13).

2. Understanding that the vocabulary of a mere mortal is limited, John does his best to describe the magnificence of the new heavens and earth in Revelation 21:1-7; 22-27. Read this passage and meditate on what is in store for all who love the Lord. Describe our final destination.

Anticipating the future glory of Jesus Christ should strengthen us during these last days. It should also purify us. John writes, "Everyone who has this hope fixed on Him purifies himself, just as He is pure" (1 John 3:3). The promise of Christ's return should serve as a powerful incentive for holy living. "Therefore, beloved, since you look for these things, be diligent to be found by Him in peace, spotless and blameless" (2 Peter 3:14). The God who called us out of darkness into His glorious light is holy. Therefore, as His image-bearers, as His earth-bound representatives, we are required to produce lives marked by "holy conduct and godliness" (2 Peter 3:11). Paul writes, "Conduct yourselves in a manner worthy of the gospel of Christ" (Philippians 1:27). Living worthy of the Lord Jesus Christ should be the full-time occupation of every believer. This spiritual discipline develops an eternal perspective, which forces us to re-evaluate the world and all its trappings and enticements.

Holy living is called for in these last days. A working knowledge of the Word of God is required in these last days. A settled faith is obligatory for these last days. A renewed mind, a surrendered will, and steadfast emotions are necessary in these last days. A strong community of likeminded believers is mandatory in these last days. While we do not know the exact day of Christ's return, we know we are nearer to the last days than any previous time in history. Soon we will be home! In the meantime, we need to stand firm. Armor up. Look up. Our redemption is drawing near!

> *Holy living is called for in these last days.*

Grow in the grace and knowledge of our Lord and Savior Jesus Christ.
To Him be the glory, both now and to the day of eternity. Amen.
2 Peter 3:18

In his second letter, Peter mentions the writings of Paul, especially those dealing with the topic of the end times. In 2 Peter 3:15-16, he writes, "According to the wisdom given him, [he] wrote to you, as also in all his letters, speaking in them of these things, in which are some things hard to understand." Even Peter acknowledged that some of Paul's writings are hard to understand. And all God's people said, "Amen!"

John MacArthur gives insight into these verses:

> However, in Paul's writings about the day of the Lord, the return of Christ, and the glories of eternity, Peter acknowledged there **are some things hard to understand,** such as the rapture of the church (1 Thessalonians 4:15–17), the coming man of sin (2 Thessalonians 2:1–4), the return of Christ in judgment (1 Thessalonians 5:1–11; 2 Thessalonians 1:3–10), and the glories of Heaven (2 Corinthians 5:1; 12:2–4). The word rendered **hard to understand** (*dusnoētos*) carries the additional connotation of "difficult to interpret." In using this term, Peter was not implying that Paul's teachings are impossible to understand. He is simply recognizing that some are more complex than others, especially prophetic revelation.[5]

These difficult topics gave ample ammunition for false teachers to teach false doctrine, disguising it with enough truth to make their lies seem plausible. Peter advises us to beware of false teachers. He refers to them as "the untaught and unstable." MacArthur explains:

> **Untaught** denotes a lack of information, and **unstable** a vacillating spiritual character. **Distort** speaks of wrenching someone's body on a torture rack. The term vividly pictures how the false teachers manipulated certain prophetic issues, twisting them to confuse and deceive the undiscerning. Such distortion often continues today regarding prophetic revelation.[6]

False teachers were prevalent in Bible times, twisting the Scriptures to pervert the message and the meaning. The same caution needs to be extended today. Not everyone teaching the Bible is speaking the truth. Some are deliberately attempting to deceive either new or ungrounded Christian converts in an effort to derail their faith. As Peter writes, "You therefore, beloved, knowing this beforehand, be on your guard so that you are not carried away by the error of unprincipled men and fall from your own steadfastness (2 Peter 3:17).

God has given the church "pastors and teachers, for the equipping of the saints for the work of service, to the building up of the body of Christ" (Ephesians 4:11). In a similar manner, Satan has false prophets and teachers to broadcast his false gospel. By distorting the Scriptures, they ensure "their own destruction" as well as the spiritual demise of their deluded followers.

Peter warns his readers lest we be "carried away" and "fall from [our] own steadfastness." Peter's concern is not that his readers will fall from salvation. (This would be contrary to the Biblical doctrine of eternal security.) Peter fears his readers will lose their spiritual equilibrium and fall from their steadfast position in Christ. Considering the escalating persecution, the enemy was leveraging any weakness in God's people, preying on their fears and undermining their confidence in the Lord. His strategical tactics are still utilized against us in spiritual warfare. Stand firm, beloved.

1. Look at 1 Corinthians 16:13. What instructions did Paul give us?

2a. Read Ephesians 4:14-15. How does Paul describe immature believers?

2b. According to this passage, what should our goal be?

Beware of false teachers. They are Satan's mouthpieces to spew his deceptions and lies. Our defensive weapon against Satan's lies is God's truth. God's truth is central to our spiritual life and essential in spiritual warfare.

His Word not only contains truth, it is Truth. The psalmist said, "The sum of Your word is truth" (Psalm 119:160). Jesus said, "I am the way, and the truth, and the life" (John 14:6). Jesus prayed for His followers, "Sanctify them in the truth; Your word is truth" (John 17:17). Jesus referred to the beloved Holy Spirit as "the Spirit of truth" (John 14:17).

God speaks truth. Satan's lies must be met with God's truth. It is the central piece of our battle weaponry in spiritual warfare. Be on guard. Your enemy wants to cause you to stumble from your steadfastness in Christ. The truth of God's Word will combat his deception and allow you to stand firm in your faith. "Therefore, my beloved brethren, be steadfast, immovable, always abounding in the work of the Lord" (1 Corinthians 15:58). Stand firm.

Peter's closing thoughts for the church before laying down his quill and rolling up his parchment was an admonition to go deeper in the things of the Lord to the glory of God. "Grow in the grace and knowledge of our Lord and Savior Jesus Christ" (2 Peter 3:18). Peter uses the full title of our Lord as he closes out his letter. Surely this was to put his readers in remembrance of our Lord's Heavenly status as well of His earthly sojourn and substitutionary sacrifice on our behalf. And he reminds his readers of God's glory. All we are and all we do is intended to bring glory to our God. Peter ends with a doxology, "To Him be the glory, both now and to the day of eternity. Amen."

As we have seen throughout this study, it is vital for us to have knowledge and insight into the way Satan works while balancing that reality with the overwhelming victory that has been granted to us through Jesus Christ our Lord. He is the Victor! Jesus has given us His Word, our external control, and His Spirit, our internal control. In Christ, we have been given authority and power over the wiles of the devil and his demons.

> *Jesus has given us His Word, our external control, and His Spirit, our internal control.*

To bring our theology into real life experience, let's look at a principle and then a practical application.

1a. Read James 1:5-8. Where will we find wisdom for all the issues of life, including spiritual warfare?

1b. Receiving God's wisdom is conditional. What is required?

God tests us; Satan tempts us. God tests us in order to strengthen us. Satan uses the flesh and the world to tempt us in order to ensnare us. The Bible clearly says, "God cannot be tempted by evil, and He Himself does not tempt anyone" (James 1:13). Satan is standing in the shadows of every enticement to sin. He uses "the lust of the flesh and the lust of the eyes and the boastful pride of life" (1 John 2:16) but he is the culprit behind every enticement to do evil. He manipulates circumstances to entice us to indulge the desires of our flesh, deeply ingrained sinful habit patterns from our life prior to Christ. His frontal attack involves our minds through our memories of the past or our anxieties about the future. He has thousands of devices for deceiving us and making sin attractive to us.

2. Look at James 1:14-15. James gives us the pattern for Satan's seduction to sin. According to this passage, how does the devil operate?

Satan cannot read our thoughts but he has been a student of human behavior since the beginning of human history. He is well aware of our vulnerabilities, both our weaknesses and strengths. He is not above attacking those areas of our strengths where we are prone to walk independent of God. "Each one is tempted when he is carried away and enticed by his own lust" (James 1:14). MacArthur notes,

> **Carried away** and **enticed** both translate participles that describe closely related but different aspects of the temptation process. The first term is from the verb *exelkō*, which has the meaning of dragging away, as if compelled by an inner desire. It was often used as a hunting term to refer to a baited trap designed to lure an unsuspecting animal into it. The second term (**enticed**) is from *deleazō*, which was commonly used as a fishing term to refer to bait, whose purpose was also to lure the prey from safety to capture and death.[7]

Satan entices our flesh. If we take the bait, we are carried away, temporarily led astray by "our own lust." That is, he entices our indwelling flesh to sin. Each of us has indwelling flesh which is tempted to respond to certain stimuli (Galatians 5:17).

As Adrian Rogers said so well:

> You cannot blame God. You cannot blame the devil. You cannot blame circumstance. The Bible says you are drawn away of your own lusts. You're absolutely free, no matter what the temptation, and it's not a sin to be tempted; you're absolutely free until the point of choice. Once you choose, once you've said, "I do," that is the consent. Now, you're free to choose, but you're not free to choose the consequences of your choice. After you choose, then your choice chooses for you.[8]

For each of us, the enticement to sin is different due to personality, environment, past life experience, and family dynamics, just to name a few. We have a unique variety of vulnerable areas which Satan exploits.

Mine is anger. I came to faith in the Lord Jesus Christ as a young married, just months before our first son was born. I would never have classified myself as an angry person until I had a child. I quickly discovered that a child who could not even form sentences had the capacity to make me very angry! By the time his little brother joined our family two years later, anger was becoming a regular occurrence, often eclipsing the mom I wanted to be to my children. A raised voice. An impatient tone. An angry countenance. I never intended anger to have a significant role in my home. Yet here it was, in danger of becoming the defining emotion of my interaction with my small children.

John MacArthur writes, "We cannot blame Satan, his demons, ungodly people, or the world in general for our **own lust.** Even more certainly, we cannot blame God. The problem is not a tempter from without, but the traitor within."[9]

About two years into my mothering career, I determined I had had enough of being ruled by such a destructive and potentially toxic emotion. I put both boys down for a nap and I had a brutally honest session with my Father, confessing my sin of anger and repenting in shame and brokenness. I asked God to teach me how to overcome this besetting sin. This led me to James 1:14-15.

God revealed to me how anger had become a besetting sin. Anger had been modeled for me. Anger had proven productive for me in getting my way and manipulating people for a favorable outcome. Anger presented itself as a friend to me. It worked in my favor. Anger was a part of my sanguine temperament. I could put all the outgoing energy of an extrovert into the avenue of anger and become volatile and explosive. I could also brood and nurse my anger, sometimes for weeks, stoking smoldering embers into a blaze. Even as a fairly young convert, I knew the sin of anger was wrong and was proving to be detrimental to the relationships of my dearest family members, my husband and my boys.

My first step was to recognize how deep-seated this issue was and how it had come to be such a stronghold in my life. I realized it had been slowly built, one brick at a time, for an extended period. Total victory would not come overnight, but the stronghold could be progressively torn down, not through behavior modification or anger management, but by the power of God!

You also may have a besetting sin, possibly different from mine, but just as dangerous, just as deadly. Name your sin and keep it in mind as I continue. Understand this, our sin may be different from other believers. This realization will keep you from comparing yourself to other believers or judging them, for they are dealing with entirely different issues than yours. Temptation comes in the form of seemingly random thoughts aimed at our particular weakness (James 1:14).

Satan speaks to us in the first person. He uses our inner voice to cause us to believe the temptation originated with us. If he used a scary monster voice or spoke to us in the third person, we would readily recognize the enemy of our soul and refuse his enticement. Dealing with the chronic response of anger, I would hear Satan's lies invading my thoughts, "I am so mad." My inner voice. My emotion. I would feel mad. My blood pressure seemed to be validating my response. I would think I had no option but to act on the thought. Frankly, I had been doing just that for 26 years. It felt familiar. It was oddly comforting. It was automatic. Consequently, I felt powerless to change a particularly devastating lie of the enemy to keep me in bondage.

Satan's enticement to sin comes to us in the form of a thought. The thought itself is not sin. However, if we cave in to it, we will be "carried away" and the thought will result in action. "Then when lust has conceived, it gives birth to sin." The thought becomes action resulting in sin and disobedience. "And when sin is accomplished, it brings forth death" (James 1:15). Not physical death, but spiritual death resulting in broken fellowship with God and with the offended party. I well remember Dr. Adrian Rogers' words, "First, sin fascinates; then, it assassinates. First, it thrills; then, it kills."[10]

This sad state does not break the relationship with God; it mars the fellowship. James adds, "Do not be deceived, my beloved brethren" (James 1:16).

How do we break the chains of bondage forged by besetting sin? How can we tear down a stronghold? How do we refuse Satan's lies? As I continued my quest to break the power of anger in my life, God led me to memorize several verses dealing with anger including James 1:19-20, "This you know, my beloved brethren. But everyone must be quick to hear, slow to speak and slow to anger; for the anger of man does not achieve the righteousness of God."

During this intensive time of awakening to the victorious Christian life, I learned I had to crucify the tempting thought BEFORE I was carried away into action. Someone irritated me. Angry thoughts flooded my mind. Obviously, these thoughts were from Satan in an effort to tempt my flesh to respond in my familiar pattern of anger. I quickly took that "thought captive to the obedience of Christ" (2 Corinthians 10:5), asked Him to crucify it, repeated my memory verses out loud, and thanked Him for the victory by faith. Having done all of this, I confidently stood on His promises of deliverance and victory. I began to praise the Lord aloud. I might add, initially I didn't feel like I had won the battle. My adrenalin was still pumping. My blood pressure was elevated. I was accustomed to moving into attack mode. Even though I did not feel in the moment like the anger had been crucified, I chose to believe the truth of God and His Word. In time, anger subsided in my life. No longer was it my go-to emotion. I had begun to realize the devastation an angry mom can wield and the damage to my personal testimony in Christ that unchecked anger could cause. Revelation 12:11 says, "They overcame [Satan] because of the blood of the Lamb and because of the word of their testimony." My testimony is "Jesus is my victory!"

Anger may or may not be your issue. But you may have one or more besetting sin issues you have not gained victory over. My hope is that through reading from my personal experience, the Holy Spirit has given you insight into any area of sin that may have you in bondage. Paul wrote, "No temptation has overtaken you but such as is common to man; and God is faithful, who will not allow you to be tempted beyond what you are able, but with the temptation will provide the way of escape also, so that you will be able to endure it" (1 Corinthians 10:13).

When Satan volleys tempting thoughts our way, we have a strategy to deal with his enticements.

1. **Recognize** that the temptation that comes through your thought life is an enticement aimed at your flesh (indwelling principle of sin).

2. **Refuse** to be carried away and enticed by your own flesh to sin. Refuse to act on it. Take the thought captive to the obedience of Christ. Ask Him to crucify it and, by any act of the will, deny its right to hold sway over you as a child of God.

3. **Run** to your stronghold, the Lord Jesus Christ. Use Scripture to denounce the power of sin in your life. By faith believe that God has done His work to crucify the sinful thought. Praise Him (aloud if it is appropriate) for allowing you to walk in victory through the power of the Holy Spirit.

Obviously, knowing how to handle God's Word is a prerequisite for dealing with any sin. If we do not know God's standard, we will not readily recognize the enticement of the evil one.

This, beloved, is how we will stand firm in the last days.

The Day of the Lord

WEEK 11 · DAY FOUR

One of Satan's most prevalent assaults in our current cultural climate, where slandering and all out hate-mongering has become the norm, is in the arena of fear. The available 24-hour news cycle in conjunction with various social media platforms has added to the atmosphere of insecurity and anxiety which are fertile ground for fear.

Louie Giglio explains:

> Fear is a giant. One of the most common giants that must fall. Fear can taunt us and harm us. Fear can get a foothold in our lives and begin to dominate us. Fear can demoralize us and ultimately diminish God's glory in our lives. It never diminishes God's glory within God himself, because God's intrinsic worth cannot be changed. But the way we reflect God's glory gets diminished. The way we show the world who God is and the way we show ourselves who God is—that's what is lessened.[11]

The Bible is replete with God's commands to "fear not," yet even for the most stalwart saint, the icy fingers of fear can creep on to derail, at least momentarily, our faith. Today we will look at a familiar Old Testament story to gain insight on dealing with one of Satan's most tried and true methods to move us from our steadfast faith in Jesus.

1. Read 1 Samuel 17:1-3. Notice the location of the Philistines' encampment. Who did the land belong to when they marshalled their forces against Israel?

Did you see it? The Philistines "gathered at Socoh which belongs to Judah." Judah was one of the tribes of Israel. The enemy was camped on land belonging to the children of God! Matthew Henry writes,

> Israel's ground would never have been footing for Philistine-armies if Israel had been faithful to their God. The Philistines (it is probable) had heard that Samuel had fallen out with Saul and forsaken him, and no longer assisted and advised him, and that Saul had grown melancholy and unfit for business, and this news encouraged them to make this attempt for the retrieving of the credit they had lately lost.[12]

The enemy camped on ground belonging to God's people! Beloved, this is such a valuable principle that relates to spiritual warfare that we must not gloss over it without grasping this truth! When we give over ground to the enemy through unconfessed sin, he will take advantage of our disobedience and set up camp on that surrendered ground!

Believers are indwelt by the Holy Spirit. Ephesians 1:13-14 says, "In Him, you also, after listening to the message of truth, the gospel of your salvation—having also believed, you were sealed in Him with the Holy Spirit of promise, who is given as a pledge of our inheritance, with the view to redemption of God's own possession, to the praise of His glory." Saved. Sealed. Safe. Having a saving relationship with Christ renders it impossible to be **possessed** by Satan. However, Satan and his demons can **oppress** believers through unconfessed sin by camping out on surrendered ground.

Jim Logan explains, "But as we've seen, Christians are already "possessed" (owned) by the Holy Spirit, so demonic possession in the sense of ownership is not the issue. Rather, the issue is the influence the evil one can exert on us."[13]

When it comes to God's people, evil spirits are spirits of influence only. That's not true for unbelievers in the world. They are held firmly in Satan's grasp, under his control, blinded in their hearts and mind and utterly dead to spiritual truth until quickened by the Holy Spirit. They are members of his kingdom of darkness.

Back to our text. "Saul and the men of Israel were gathered…and drew up in battle array to encounter the Philistines." Beloved, the Christian life is a battle against "rulers, against the powers, against the world forces of this darkness, against the spiritual forces of wickedness in heavenly places" (Ephesians 6:12). The battle is raging. Whether you armor up and show up is totally up to you. It is here in our text we are introduced to the Philistines' champion.

2. Read 1 Samuel 17:4-11. Describe Goliath.

3. What was Goliath's taunt toward the Israelites?

4. What was the result of Goliath's jeers in the Israelites' camp?

Satan and his forces used fear to paralyze God's people who have the promise of victory. Meanwhile, David who "was the son of the Ephrathite of Bethlehem in Judah" (1 Samuel 17:12) is tending "his father's flock in Bethlehem" (1 Samuel 17:14).

David is an Old Testament picture or type of Christ. Three of David's older brothers "had gone after Saul to the battle" (1 Samuel 17:13). Goliath "came forward morning and evening for forty days and took his stand" (1 Samuel 17:16). Don't miss this nugget. Forty days is the same amount of time Jesus was tempted by Satan in the wilderness, an Old Testament picture of a New Testament account of the life of our Lord as He engaged in spiritual warfare with the devil.

David's father sent him to take provisions to his brothers. "So David arose early in the morning and left the flock with a keeper and took the supplies and went as [his father] Jesse had commanded him" (1 Samuel 17:20). David was tending sheep. The father sent David to the front lines. Just as David's routine was interrupted by his father to engage in the enemy's activity, we are to be armored up at all times, ready to do battle. David left his flock, his work, and entered the battle fray at his father's command. Beloved, armor up and stay at the ready!

As David was greeting his brothers, Goliath began mocking the Israelites and their God. Notice the progression of Israel's exposure to Goliath. First "Saul and all Israel heard these words of the Philistine, [and] they were dismayed and greatly afraid" (1 Samuel 17:11). Goliath's words were enough to strike fear in the hearts of seasoned Israelite warriors. Then, "Israel and the Philistines drew up in battle array, army against army…when all the men of Israel saw the man, they fled from him and were greatly afraid" (I Samuel 17:21,24). Now the whole army, the rank and file, got a good close look at Goliath. He was more powerful, more intimidating, and much more frightening then they had even imagined and "they fled from him and were greatly afraid." Goliath was emboldened and his influence more impactful the longer the Israelites refused to attack their enemy.

Matthew Henry explains,

> Forty days the two armies lay encamped facing one another, each advantageously posted, but neither forward to engage. Either they were parleying and treating of an accommodation or they were waiting for recruits; and perhaps there were frequent skirmishes between small detached parties. All this while, twice a day, morning and evening, did the insulting champion appear in the field and repeat his challenge, his own heart growing more and more proud for his not being answered and the people of Israel more and more timorous, while God designed hereby to ripen him for destruction and to make Israel's deliverance the more illustrious.[14]

Beloved, Satan and his army gain influence in our lives the longer we allow unconfessed sin to remain unchecked in our lives. Such shortsightedness causes us to wander from the spiritual disciplines that increase our faith. Spending time in the Word with the Lord every day, memorizing and meditating on the Word, regularly connecting with believers in corporate worship in a Bible-believing local church, exposing ourselves to solid Bible preaching and teaching, building strong relationships with fellow believers, fellowshipping with likeminded believers in the community of Christ, being discipled and poured into by a more mature Christian for the purpose of becoming a disciple-maker, and pursuing the things of God are just some of the ways we "grow in the grace and knowledge of the Lord and Savior Jesus Christ" (2 Peter 3:18). These disciplines strengthen our faith and ready us for spiritual warfare. Later David would write, "Blessed be the Lord, my rock, who trains my hands for war, and my fingers for battle" (Psalm 144:1). Could it be that David was thinking of his epic battle against Goliath when he penned these words? I'd like to think so!

5. Read 1 Samuel 17:31-37. David approached King Saul to announce his intention of fighting the champion. The king assured David his age naturally disqualified him from the fight. What was David's response to King Saul?

David's declaration of faith in God's ability to overcome Israel's enemy based on past victories emboldened him to stand strong in his present circumstances. We should stand confidently in the promises of God, remembering His past faithfulness even as we reckon on His victory in our current battle.

King Saul insisted David wear the king's armor. David rejected the over-sized armor in favor of his tried and tested implements. "He took his stick in his hand and chose for himself five smooth stones from the brook, and put them in the shepherd's bag which he had, even in his pouch, and his sling was in his hand; and he approached the Philistine" (1 Samuel 17:40). As we have seen, God has given each of us the whole armor of God, perfectly suited for our battles.

6. Read 1 Samuel 17:41-51. Goliath "cursed David by his gods." What was David's response?

7. Describe David's victory.

8. What happened to the Philistines when they saw their champion was dead?

9. Reflect on the story of David and Goliath. What applications can you glean in regard to spiritual warfare?

As we fight the good fight of faith, we come against Satan and his demons "in the name of the Lord of hosts, the God of the armies of Israel" (1 Samuel 17:45). Beloved, learn this glorious truth. "The Lord does not deliver by sword or by spear; for the battle is the Lord's" (1 Samuel 17:47). He will fight for you! So, armor up and stand firm in these last days.

Congratulations! We have come to the end of our study. I must admit, I will miss my daily encounters with Peter. He has become a dear friend, a trustworthy mentor, and an ally in spiritual warfare through his instructions and admonitions. I am most encouraged by Peter's testimony for the Lord. Adrian Rogers writes,

> Simon Peter knew what it was to be swallowed down by the enemy, didn't he? Simon Peter was sleeping when he should have been praying. And then, when the enemy came into the garden to take Jesus, Simon Peter reached up, drew his sword, smote off the ear of Malchus, the servant of the high priest, trying to do spiritual work in the energy of the flesh. All he did was to do a poor job of swordsmanship and mess up the whole deal and give the name of Jesus a bad reputation. The weapons of our warfare are not carnal, but spiritual. Later on, on the Day of Pentecost, he used the sword of the Spirit and slew 3,000, but only cut them alive and not cut them dead, and brought them to the Lord Jesus Christ.[15]

Peter battled his own flesh. He was impulsive, self-centered, and double-minded at times. He disobeyed the Lord. He even denied the Lord, but that's not the end of his story. Jesus forgave Peter, restored him to service (see John 21:15-17), and used him dramatically in Kingdom work (see Acts 2:1-38). Who could better teach us about the schemes of the devil than Peter? We must take his words to heart and walk in obedience to God's Word, dependence on God's Spirit, and confidence in the completed work of Jesus Christ on our behalf. Simon Peter did not start well, but he finished strong. I intend to do likewise!

1. Read 1 John 2:12-14. Notice the progression of groups John is addressing—little children, young men, and fathers. John reminds us of the legitimacy of each season of spiritual growth. What body of truth has each group amassed? Put a star by where you think you are in your walk with the Lord.

   a. little children

   b. young men

   c. fathers

2. Take a moment for some personal reflection. What practical steps can you (will you) take to advance to the next level of spiritual maturity?

John affirms each group for the depth of spiritual maturity they have, acknowledging the progressive nature of growing in Christ, which is often referred to as sanctification. In 1 Corinthians 13:11 Paul writes, "When I was a child, I used to speak like a child, think like a child, reason like a child; when I became a man, I did away with childish things." Spiritual growth is very similar to physical development. Healthy physical growth is marked by stages of development. Each stage is to lead to the next level of maturity. The progression is slow and often painful, but the end result is a mature adult who is socially, mentally, and emotionally stable. Likewise, in the spiritual realm we are to mature—regardless of our age—from a new convert to a baby Christian, to an adolescent, to a young person, and on to a spiritually maturing adult. Obviously, we never arrive to full maturity in this life, but we should continue to grow in our faith until we see Jesus. "For now we see in a mirror dimly, but then face to face; now I know in part, but then I will know fully just as I also have been fully known (1 Corinthians 13:12). My encouragement to you is that, whatever age or stage you are currently in, you continue to "grow in the grace and knowledge of our Lord and Savior Jesus Christ" (2 Peter 3:18).

As we reach the end of this study, let me ask once again, "Do you know Jesus Christ as your personal Lord and Savior? Has there ever been a time when you invited Him to be your Lord and Savior?" Gaining insight on Satan's diabolical schemes will do you little good if you have never come to a place of repentance and faith. Your eternal destination in either heaven or hell rests on whether you receive Jesus or reject Jesus in this life.

3. Please read 1 John 3:4-10. What is the pattern of living, the lifestyle of those who have a personal relationship with Jesus Christ?

4. How does John identify those who are outside a personal relationship with Jesus?

Jesus said, "What does it profit a man to gain the whole world, and forfeit his soul?" (Mark 8:36). What would it profit you to complete a study on spiritual warfare without coming to the saving knowledge of Jesus Christ, our Victor! In the appendix of this study, you will find a guide that will walk you through the steps to invite Christ into your life.

While only God can know the true condition of the heart, the one who loves the Lord will "practice righteousness" despite momentary lapses into sin. The one who does not know the Lord will reveal their spiritual condition by living a life marked by habitually behaving in ways that are inconsistent with God's divine written revelation.

Those who belong to Jesus pursue holy living.

Those who belong to Jesus pursue holy living. They are capable of sin, but the overarching theme of their lifestyle speaks to a commitment to Christ and spiritual growth. John wrote, "By this we know that we have come to know Him, if we keep his commandments" (1 John 2:3). The word "keep" is a nautical term. Sailors in Bible times lacked sophisticated instruments. They set their course by "keeping the stars." Believers set the course of their lives according to God's Word. As Adrian Rogers said,

Now, the Bible says if we know Him, we are going to keep His commandments— we're going to steer by God's stars, as it were. We're going to keep His Word. That doesn't mean that a sailor could not get blown off course; that doesn't mean in a time of distraction, he might mis-turn the wheel. But, it does mean that he has a guide for his life; he has a direction that he's going; he has a fixed standard that he's living by.[16]

We too have a fixed standard to live by: the inerrant, infallible Word of God. Through the intentional and consistent study of God's Word, we learn how to walk in obedience and live out the reality of Christ through the power in His indwelling Holy Spirit. May God bless you as you pursue a life of personal holiness and practical righteousness.

And may you be strengthened in your faith, committed in your prayer life, dedicated to the study of God's Word, educated about the workings of our enemy, and engaged in spiritual warfare as you stand firm in the last days.

Grow in the grace and knowledge of our Lord and Savior
Jesus Christ. To Him be the glory, both now and
To the day of eternity. Amen.
2 Peter 3:18

How to Become a Christian

Dear one, has there ever been a time that you have given your heart to the Lord? Do you have the assurance that if you were to die right now, you would go straight to heaven to spend all eternity in the presence of the Lord Jesus Christ and all His followers? If not, please let me share with you how you can be saved.

Admit Your Sin

First, you must understand that you are a sinner. The Bible says, *All have sinned and fall short of the glory of God* (Rom. 3:23). In Romans 6:23 the Bible says, *For the wages of sin is death.* That means that sin has separated us from a Holy God and we are under the sentence of eternal death and separation from God.

Abandon Self-Effort

Secondly, you must understand that you cannot save yourself by your own efforts. The Bible is very clear that it is *not by works of righteousness which we have done, but according to His mercy He saved us* (Titus 3:5). Again, in Ephesians 2:8-9 the Bible says, *For by grace you have been saved through faith; and that not of yourselves, it is the gift of God; not as a result of works, that no one should boast.*

Acknowledge Christ's Payment

Thirdly, you must believe that Jesus Christ, the Son of God, died for your sins. The Bible says, *God demonstrates His own love toward us, in that while we were yet sinners, Christ died for us* (Rom. 5:8). That means He died a sacrificial death in your place. Your sin debt has been paid by the blood of Jesus Christ, which *cleanses us from all sin* (I John 1:7).

Accept Him as Savior

Fourthly, you must put your faith in Jesus Christ and Him alone for your salvation. The blood of Christ does you no good until you receive Him by faith. The Bible says, *Believe on the Lord Jesus Christ, and you shall be saved* (Acts 16:31).

Has there been a time in your life that you have taken this all-important step of faith? If not, I urge you to do it right now. Jesus Christ is the only way to heaven. He said, *"I am the way, the truth, and the life; no man comes unto the Father, but by Me"* (John 14:16).

Would you like to become a Christian? Would you like to invite Jesus Christ to come into your heart today? Read over this prayer and if it expresses the desire of your heart, you may ask Him into your heart to take away your sin, fill you with His Spirit, and take you to home to heaven when you die. If this is your intention, pray this prayer.

"Oh God, I'm a sinner. I am lost and I need to be saved. I know I cannot save myself, so right now, once and for all, I trust You to save me. Come into my heart, forgive my sin, and make me Your child. I give you my life. I will live for You as You give me Your strength. Amen"

If you will make this your heartfelt prayer, God will hear and save you! Jesus has promised that He will never leave nor forsake anyone who comes to Him in faith. In John 6:37 He said, *"The One who comes to Me I will certainly not cast out."*

Welcome to the family!

End Notes

Introduction

1. Milton, J. (2000). *Paradise Lost (Classics, 1ˢᵗ Edition)*, p. 91. New York, NY: Penguin Putnam.

2. Moskowitz, C. (May 12, 2011). *Space.com*. Retrieved from https://www.space.com/11642-dark-matter-dark-energy-4-percent-universe-panek.html

3. Ingram, C. (2006). *The Invisible War*, pp. 33-34. Grand Rapids, MI: Baker Books.

4. Sun Tzu & Griffith, S. B. (1964). *The Art of War*, p. 28. Oxford: Clarendon Press.

5. Stedman, R. (1999). *Spiritual Warfare*, pp. 192-193. Grand Rapids, MI: Discovery House Publishers.

6. Rippon, J. (1956). How Firm a Foundation. *The Baptist Hymnal*, p. 263. Nashville, TN: Convention Press.

Week 1

1. Wheaton, D. H. (1994). 2 Peter. D. A. Carson, R. T. France, J. A. Motyer, & G. J. Wenham (Eds.), *New Bible Commentary: 21ˢᵗ Century Edition* (4ᵗʰ ed., p. 1389). Leicester, England; Downers Grove, IL: Inter-varsity Press.

2. Wheaton, D. H. (1994). 2 Peter. D. A. Carson, R. T. France, J. A. Motyer, & G. J. Wenham (Eds.), *New Bible Commentary: 21ˢᵗ Century Edition* (4ᵗʰ ed., p. 1388). Leicester, England; Downers Grove, IL: Inter-varsity Press.

3. Hindson, E., Caner, E. (2008). *The Popular Encyclopedia of Apologetics*, p. 121. Eugene, OR: Harvest House Publishers.

4. Hindson, E., Caner, E. (2008). *The Popular Encyclopedia of Apologetics*, p. 122. Eugene, OR: Harvest House Publishers.

5. Hindson, E., Caner, E. (2008). *The Popular Encyclopedia of Apologetics*, p. 123. Eugene, OR: Harvest House Publishers.

6. Demarest B., Matthews, K. (2010). *Dictionary of Everyday Theology and Culture*, p. 433. Colorado Springs, CO: Navpress.

7. Demarest B., Matthews, K. (2010). *Dictionary of Everyday Theology and Culture*, p. 433. Colorado Springs, CO: Navpress.

8. Hindson, E., Caner, E. (2008). *The Popular Encyclopedia of Apologetics*, p. 499. Eugene, OR: Harvest House Publishers.

9. McDowell, J., & McDowell, S. (2010). *The Unshakable Truth*, p. 353. Eugene, OR: Harvest House Publishers.

10. Hindson, E., Caner, E. (2008). *The Popular Encyclopedia of Apologetics*, p. 125. Eugene, OR: Harvest House Publishers.

11. McDowell, J., McDowell, S. (2010). *The Unshakable Truth*, p. 258. Eugene, OR: Harvest House Publishers.

12. McDowell, J., McDowell, S. (2010). *The Unshakable Truth*, p. 257. Eugene, OR: Harvest House Publishers.

13. McDowell, J., McDowell, S. (2010). *The Unshakable Truth*, p. 262. Eugene, OR: Harvest House Publishers.

14. Dean, J. K., (2012). *Altar'd*, p. 91. Birmingham, AL: New Hope Publishers

15. McGee, R. (1985). *The Search for Significance*, p. 152-153. Nashville, TN: Lifeway Christian Resources.

16. Spurgeon, C. (1993). *Spiritual Warfare in a Believer's Life*, p. 56. Lynnwood, WA: Emerald Books.

17. Logan, J. (1995). *Reclaiming Surrendered Ground*, p.190. Chicago, IL: Moody Publishers.

18. McGee, R. (1985). *The Search for Significance*, p. 158-159. Nashville, TN: Lifeway Christian Resources.

19. McGee, R. (1985). *The Search for Significance*, p. 159. Nashville, TN: Lifeway Christian Resources

20. Carter, R. K. (1886). Standing on the Promises. *The Baptist Hymnal*, p. 266. Nashville, TN: Convention Press

Week 2

1. Shirer, P. *Fervent: A Woman's Battle Plan to Serious, Specific, and Strategic Prayer*, p. 25. Nashville, TN: B&H Publishing Group.

2. MacArthur, J. F., Jr. (2005). *2 Peter and Jude*, p. 44. Chicago, IL: Moody Publishers.

3. Wiersbe, W. W. (1996). *The Strategy of Satan: How to Detect and Defeat Him*, p. 23. Wheaton, IL: Tyndale House Publishers.

4. Evans, T. *Victory in Spiritual Warfare: Outfitting Yourself for the Battle*, pp. 14-15. Eugene, OR: Harvest House Publishers.

5. Wiersbe, W. W. (1996). *The Strategy of Satan: How to Detect and Defeat Him*, p. 11. Wheaton, IL: Tyndale House Publishers.

6. MacArthur, J. (2005). *Twelve Extraordinary Women*, pp. 76-77. Nashville, TN: Thomas Nelson, Inc.

7. MacArthur, J. (2005). *Twelve Extraordinary Women*, p. 77. Nashville, TN: Thomas Nelson, Inc.

8. James, C. C. (2008). *The Gospel of Ruth: Loving God Enough to Break the Rules*, p. 96. Grand Rapids, MI: Zondervan.

9. Rogers, A. (2017). The Triumph of Faith. In *Adrian Rogers Sermon Archive* (Jos 5:13–15). Signal Hill, CA: Rogers Family Trust.

10. Wiersbe, W. W. (1996). *The Strategy of Satan: How to Detect and Defeat Him*, p. 96. Wheaton, IL: Tyndale House Publishers.

11. Rogers, A. (2017). The Sin that Lost a War. In *Adrian Rogers Sermon Archive* (Jos 7). Signal Hill, CA: Rogers Family Trust.

Week 3

1. Swindoll, C. R. (n.d.) *Insight.org*. Retrieved from https://www.insight.org/resources/daily-devotional/individual/the-majesty-of-god

2. Swindoll, C. R. (n.d.) *Insight.org*. Retrieved from https://www.insight.org/resources/daily-devotional/individual/the-majesty-of-god

3. *Life Application Study Bible, New Living Translation,* (2007). p. 2799. Carol Stream, IL: Tyndale House Publishers, Inc.

4. Tozer, A.W. (1961). *The Knowledge of the Holy*, p. 2. New York, NY: Harper Collins Publishers.

5. Tozer, A.W. (1961). *The Knowledge of the Holy*, p. 1. New York, NY: Harper Collins Publishers.

6. Gunter, S. (1995). *Prayer Portions*, p. 45. Birmingham, AL: The Father's Business.

7. Evans, T. (2011). *Victory in Spiritual Warfare*, p. 29. Eugene, OR: Harvest House Publishers.

8. Gunter, S. (1995). *Prayer Portions*, p. 45. Birmingham, AL: The Father's Business.

9. Gunter, S. (1995). *Prayer Portions*, p. 45. Birmingham, AL: The Father's Business.

10. Graham, B. (n.d.). *Billy Graham*, Retrieved from https://billygraham.org/answer/is-god-in-the-details/.

11. Gunter, S. (1995). *Prayer Portions*, p. 47. Birmingham, AL: The Father's Business.

12. Mohler, A. (n.d.). *Ligonier*. Retrieved from https://www.ligonier.org/learn/articles/christ-victor/

13. Evans, T. (2011). *Victory in Spiritual Warfare*, pp. 41-42. Eugene, OR: Harvest House Publishers.

14. Evans, T. (2011). *Victory in Spiritual Warfare*, pp 34-35. Eugene, OR: Harvest House Publishers.

15. Graham, B. (n.d.). *Billy Graham*. Retrieved from https://billygraham.org/decision-magazine/april-2007/victorious-christian-living/

16. Zschech, D. (n.d.). *AZ Lyrics*. Victor's Crown. Retrieved from https://www.azlyrics.com/lyrics/darlenezschech/victorscrown.html

Week 4

1. Ingram, C. (2006). *The Invisible War*, p. 43. Grand Rapids, MI: Baker Books.

2. Ingram, C. (2006). *The Invisible War*, p. 46. Grand Rapids, MI: Baker Books.

3. Lewis, C.S. (1980). *Mere Christianity*, p. 49. New York, NY: Harper Collins Publishers.

4. MacArthur, J. (2005). *2 Peter and Jude New Testament Commentary*, p. 67. Chicago, IL: Moody Publishers.

5. Heresies. (n.d.) *Vines Expository Dictionary of NT Words*. Retrieved from https://www.studylight.org/dictionaries/ved/h/heresy.html?hilite=heresies

6. MacArthur, J. (2005). *2 Peter and Jude New Testament Commentary*, p. 72. Chicago, IL: Moody Publishers.

7. Bonhoeffer, D. (1955) *Temptation*, p. 25. London: SCM Press.

8. Ingram, C. (2006). *The Invisible War*, p. 47. Grand Rapids, MI: Baker Books.

9. Luther, M. A Mighty Fortress is Our God. *The Baptist Hymnal*, p. 40. Nashville, TN: Convention Press.

10. Stedman, R. (1975). *Spiritual Warfare: How to Stand Firm in the Faith*, p. Loc. 552. Discovery House Publishers.

11. Gunter, S. (1995). *Prayer Portions*, p. 287. Birmingham, AL: The Father's Business.

12. Bridges, Jerry. (2006). *The Pursuit of Holiness*, p. 16. Colorado Springs, CO: Navpress.

13. Evans, T. (1995). *Victory in Spiritual Warfare: Outfitting Yourself for the Battle*, p. 19. Eugene, OR: Harvest House Publishers.

14. Shirer, P. (2015). *Fervent*, p. 81. Nashville, TN: B & H Publishing Group.

Week 5

1. Tozer, A.W. (1993). *The Warfare of the Spirit*, pp. 133-134. Chicago, IL: Wingspread Publishers.

2. Willard, D. (1998). *The Divine Conspiracy*, p. 47. New York, NY: Harper Collins Publishers.

3. Lewis, C.S. (1980). *Mere Christianity*, p. 123. New York, NY: Harper Collins Publishers.

4. Wagner, K. (2012). *Fierce Women*, p. 85. Chicago, IL: Moody Publishers.

5. Tozer, A.W. (1994). *Tozer Speaks: Volume One*, p. 212. Camp Hill, PA: WingSpread Publishers.

6. MacArthur, J.F., Jr. (2005). *2 Peter and Jude*, p. 98. Chicago, IL: Moody Publishers.

7. Warner, T. (1991). *Spiritual Warfare*, p. 79. Wheaton, IL: Crossway.

8. Tozer, A.W. (July 29, 2018). *The Alliance Tozer Devotional.* Retrieved from https://www.cmalliance.org/devotions/tozer?id=1252

9. Bubeck, M. (2013). *The Adversary*, p. 28. Chicago, IL: Moody Press.

10. Wiersbe, W. (1975). *Be Free*, p. 129. Wheaton, IL: Victor Books.

11. *New York Times*. (February 17, 1862). Retrieved from https://www.nytimes.com/1862/02/17/archives/the-fort-donelson-battle-reports-of-three-days-desperate.html

12. Piper, J. (April 26, 1981). The Sifting of Simon Peter. *Desiring God*. Retrieved from https://www.desiringgod.org/messages/the-sifting-of-simon-peter

13. Green, J. (1997). *The New International Commentary on the New Testament*, p. 771. Grand Rapids, MI: Wm B. Eerdmans Publishing.

14. Wiersbe, W. (1977). *Be Rich*, p. 163. Wheaton, IL: Victor Books.

15. Sorge, B. (2000). *Glory: When Heaven Invades Earth*, p. 75. Greenwood, MO: Oasis House.

16. Roosevelt, T. (n.d.) The Strenuous Life. *Voices of Democracy*. Retrieved from http://voicesofdemocracy.umd.edu/roosevelt-strenuous-life-1899-speech-text/

17. Resist. (n.d.). *Vine's Expository Dictionary of NT Words*. Retrieved from https://www.studylight. org/dictionaries/ved/r/resist.html?hilite=resist

18. Hodge, C. (n.d.). *Commentary on Ephesians*, p. 380-381. Old Tappan, NJ: Fleming Revell Company.

19. Principality. (n.d.). *Vine's Expository Dictionary of NT Words*. Retrieved from https://www. studylight.org/dictionaries/ved/p/principality.html?hilite=Principalities

20. Powers. (n.d.). *Vine's Expository Dictionary of NT Words*. Retrieved from https://www.studylight. org/dictionaries/ved/h/heaven-heavenly.html?hilite=powers

21. High Places. (n.d.). *Vine's Expository Dictionary of NT Words*. Retrieved from https://www. studylight.org/dictionaries/ved/h/high-highly.html?hilite=high%20places

22. Evans, T. (2011). *Victory in Spiritual Warfare*, p. 15. Eugene, OR: Harvest House Publishers.

23. Anonymous. (September 4, 2002). *Baptist Press*. Retrieved from http://www.bpnews.net/14164/ soldiers-pledge

24. Lewis, C.S. (1996). *The Screwtape Letters*, p. 105. New York, NY: Harper Collins.

25. MacArthur, J.F., Jr. (1986). *Ephesians*, pp. 350-351. Chicago, IL: Moody Publishers.

Week 6

1. Luther, M. (n.d.). In Defense of All the Articles. *God Rules*. Retrieved from http://www.godrules. net/library/luther/NEW1luther_c4.htm

2. MacArthur, J.F., Jr. (1986). *Ephesians*, p. 351. Chicago, IL: Moody Publishers.

3. MacArthur, J.F., Jr. (1986). *Ephesians*, p. 351. Chicago, IL: Moody Publishers.

4. Evans, T. (2011). *Victory in Spiritual Warfare*, p. 67. Eugene, OR: Harvest House Publishers.

5. Evans, T. (2011). *Victory in Spiritual Warfare*, pp. 67-68. Eugene, OR: Harvest House Publishers.

6. MacArthur, J.F., Jr. (1986). *Ephesians*, p. 353. Chicago, IL: Moody Publishers.

7. Mote, E. (1956). The Solid Rock. *The Baptist Hymnal*, p. 283. Nashville, TN: Convention Press.

8. MacArthur, J.F., Jr. (1986). *Ephesians*, p. 354. Chicago, IL: Moody Publishers.

9. Evans, T. (2011). *Victory in Spiritual Warfare*, p. 78. Eugene, OR: Harvest House Publishers.

10. Bruce, F.F. (1984). *The Epistles to the Colossians, to Philemon, and to the Ephesians*, p. 408. Grand Rapids, MI: William B. Eerdmans Publishing.

11. Evans, T. (2011). *Victory in Spiritual Warfare: Field Guide for Battle*, p. 93. Nashville, TN: B&H Publishing Group.

12. Spurgeon, C. H. (n.d). The Shield of Faith. *Christian Classics Ethereal Library*. Retrieved from https://www.ccel.org/ccel/spurgeon/sermons07.lx.html

13. MacArthur, J.F., Jr. (1986). *Ephesians*, p. 358. Chicago, IL: Moody Publishers.

14. Lloyd-Jones, D.M. (1977). *The Christian Soldier*, p. 305. Grand Rapids, MI: Baker Books.

15. Sproul, R.C. (2009). *Surprised by Suffering: The Role of Pain and Death in the Christian Life*, p. 88. Harrisonburg, VA: Tyndale House Publishing.

16. MacArthur, J.F., Jr. (1986). *Ephesians*, p. 358. Chicago, IL: Moody Publishers.

17. Shirer, P. (2015). *The Armor of God*, p. 127. Nashville, TN: Lifeway Church Resources.

18. Spurgeon, C. H. (n.d). The Shield of Faith. *Christian Classics Ethereal Library*. Retrieved from https://www.ccel.org/ccel/spurgeon/sermons07.lx.html

19. Spurgeon, C. H. (n.d). The Shield of Faith. *Christian Classics Ethereal Library*. Retrieved from https://www.ccel.org/ccel/spurgeon/sermons07.lx.html

20. MacArthur, J.F., Jr. (June 3, 1979). The Believer's Armor, Part 5. *Grace to You*. https://www.gty.org/library/sermons-library/1959/the-believers-armor-part-5-the-helmet-of-salvation-part-1

21. Duffield, G. (1956). Stand Up, Stand Up for Jesus. *The Baptist Hymnal*, p. 415. Nashville, TN: Convention Press.

22. MacArthur, J.F., Jr. (1986). *Ephesians*, p. 367-368. Chicago, IL: Moody Publishers.

23. Cole, S. (n.d.). The Weapon. *Bible.org*. Retrieved from https://bible.org/seriespage/lesson-61-weapon-ephesians-617b

24. Spurgeon, C. H. (1875). *The Metropolitan Tabernacle Pulpit*, p. 703. London: Passamore and Alabaster.

25. Guthrie, T. (n.d.). *The Way to Life*, p. 91. London: Palala Press.

26. Rogers, A. (n.d.). From sermon notes taken by Bill Street.

27. MacArthur, J.F., Jr. (1986). *Ephesians*, p. 368. Chicago, IL: Moody Publishers.

28. Mears, H. (1966). *What the Bible is All About*, p. 518. Ventura, CA: Regal Books.

Week 7

1. Stedman, R. (1999). *Spiritual Warfare: How to Stand Firm in the Faith*, p. 40. Grand Rapids, MI: Discovery House.

2. Anderson, N. & Warner, T. (2000). *The Beginner's Guide to Spiritual Warfare*, p. 39. Ventura, CA: Regal Books.

3. Strong, J. (2007). *Strong's Exhaustive Concordance of the Bible*, p. 211. Peabody, MA: Hendrickson Publishers.

4. Weaver, V. (November 5, 2018). Re: Message to Donna Gaines.

5. Ingram, C. (2006). *The Invisible War*, p.137. Grand Rapids, MI: Baker Books.

6. Ingram, C. (2006). *The Invisible War*, p.137. Grand Rapids, MI: Baker Books.

7. Rankin, J. (2009). *Spiritual Warfare: The Battle for God's Glory*, p. 124. Nashville, TN: B&H Publishing Group.

8. Arthur, K. (2011). *As Silver Refined: Answers to Life's Disappointments*, p. 55. Colorado Springs, CO: WaterBrook Press

9. Moore, B. (2009). *Praying God's Word: Breaking Free from Spiritual Strongholds*, p. 15. Nashville, TN: B&H Publishing Group.

10. Logan, J. (1995). *Reclaiming Surrendered Ground: Protecting Your Family from Spiritual Attacks*, pp. 34-35. Chicago, IL: Moody Publishers.

Week 8

1. Logan, J. (1995). *Reclaiming Surrendered Ground*, p. 13. Chicago, IL: Moody Publishers.

2. Logan, J. (1995). *Reclaiming Surrendered Ground*, p. 15. Chicago, IL: Moody Publishers.

3. Gunter, S. (1995). *Prayer Portions*, p. 45. Birmingham, AL: The Father's Business.

4. Gunter, Sylvia. (1995). *Prayer Portions*, p. 45. Birmingham, AL: The Father's Business.

5. Gaines, S. (2013). *Pray Like It Matters*, p. 13. Tigerville, SC: Auxano Press.

6. Velarde, R. (n.d.). *Focus on the Family*. Retrieved from https://www.focusonthefamily.com/faith/faith-in-life/prayer/prayer

7. Logan, J. (1995). *Reclaiming Surrendered Ground*, p. 157. Chicago, IL: Moody Publishers.

8. McKernan, B. (n.d.). *Desiring God.* Retrieved from https://www. desiringgod.org/articles/seven-steps-to- strengthen-prayer.

9. Logan, J. (1995). *Reclaiming Surrendered Ground*, p. 165. Chicago, IL: Moody Publishers.

10. Logan, J. (1995). *Reclaiming Surrendered Ground*, p. 157. Chicago, IL: Moody Publishers.

11. Hall, J. H. (n.d.). *Bible.org.* Retrieved from https://blog.bible.org/ illustration/james-516

12. Gunter, S. (1994). *For the Family*, p. 19. Birmingham, AL: The Father's Business.

13. *Revive Our Hearts.* (n.d.). Retrieved from https://www.reviveourhearts.com/articles/31-days-of-praying-for-your- husband/.

14. *Loving Life at Home.* (n.d.). Pray for Your Husband from Head to Toe. Retrieved from https:// lovinglifeathome.com/2013/08/01/praying-for-your-husband-from-head-to-toe/

15. Gunter, S. (1994). *For the Family*, p. 19. Birmingham, AL: The Father's Business.

16. Batterson, M. (2012). *Praying Circles Around Your Children*, p. 11. Grand Rapids, MI: Zondervan.

17. Omartian, S. (1995). *The Power of a Praying Parent*, p. 29. Eugene, OR: Harvest House Publishers.

18. Batterson, M. (2012). *Praying Circles Around Your Children*, p. 26. Grand Rapids, MI: Zondervan.

19. Evans, T. (2011). *Victory in Spiritual Warfare*, p.146 Eugene, OR: Harvest House Publishers.

20. Batterson, M. (2012). *Praying Circles Around Your Children*, p. 9. Grand Rapids, MI: Zondervan.

21. Evans, T. (2011). *Victory in Spiritual Warfare*, p. 147. Eugene, OR: Harvest House Publishers.

22. Logan, J. (1995). *Reclaiming Surrendered Ground*, p. 175. Chicago, IL: Moody Publishers.

23. Piper, J. (n.d.). *Desiring God.* Retrieved from https://www.desiringgod.org/interviews/when-should-i-stop-praying-for-something

24. Shirer, P. (n.d.). *Lifeway.* Retrieved from https://www.lifeway.com/en/articles/how-to-pray-for-your-family

25. Evans, T. (2011). *Victory in Spiritual Warfare*, p. 146. Eugene, OR: Harvest House Publishers.

26. *Focus on the Family.* (n.d.). Retrieved from https://www.focusonthefamily.com/family-q-and-a/ parenting/praying-together-as-a-family

27. Evans, T. (2011). *Victory in Spiritual Warfare*, p.137. Eugene, OR: Harvest House Publishers.

Week 9

1. Logan, J. (1995). *Reclaiming Surrendered Ground*, p. 42. Chicago, IL: Moody Publishers.

2. Moore, B. (2009). *Praying God's Word*, p. 325. Nashville, TN: B&H Publishing.

3. Moore, R. (2015). *Onward: Engaging the Culture Without Losing the Gospel*, p. 10. Nashville, TN: B&H Publishing.

4. Gunter, S. (1995). *Prayer Portions*, p. 304. Birmingham, AL: The Father's Business.

5. Moore, B. (2009). *Praying God's Word*, p. 16. Nashville, TN: B&H Publishing.

Week 10

1. Rogers, A. (2013). *Unveiling The End Times In Our Time*, p. x. Nashville, TN: B & H Publishing Group.

2. Wiersbe, W. (1989). *The Bible Exposition Commentary, Volume 2*, p. 462. Wheaton, IL: Victor Books.

3. Wiersbe, W. (1989). *The Bible Exposition Commentary, Volume 2*, p. 463. Wheaton, IL: Victor Books.

4. Wiersbe, W. (1989). *The Bible Exposition Commentary, Volume 2*, p. 463. Wheaton, IL: Victor Books.

5. Patterson, D., Kelley, R. (2006). *Women's Evangelical Commentary New Testament*, p. 855. Nashville, TN: Broadman and Holman Publishers.

6. Jeremiah, D. (2016). *Is This The End*, p. 243. Nashville, TN: W Publishing Group.

7. Wiersbe, W. (1989). *The Bible Exposition Commentary, Volume 1*, p. 89. Wheaton, IL: Victor Books.

8. Rogers, A. (2013). *Unveiling The End Times In Our Time*, p. xi. Nashville, TN: B & H Publishing Group.

9. Jeremiah, D. (1999). *Jesus' Final Warning*, p. 39. Nashville, TN: Word Publishing.

10. Jeremiah, D. (1999). *Jesus' Final Warning*, p. 31. Nashville, TN: Word Publishing.

11. Jeremiah, D. (2016). *Is This The End*, p. 15. Nashville, TN: W Publishing Group.

12. Jeremiah, D. (2008). *What in the World Is Going On?*, p. 135-136. Nashville, TN: Thomas Nelson.

13. Jeremiah, D. (2016). *Is This The End*, p. 61-65. Nashville, TN: W Publishing Group.

14. Tackett, D. (October 27, 2016). *Focus on the Family*. Christian Worldview. Retrieved from http://www.focusonthefamily.com/faith/Christian-worldview/what-a-christian-worldview10-27-2016

15. Jeremiah, D. (2016). *Is This The End*, p. 72. Nashville, TN: W Publishing Group.

16. Rogers, A. (2002). *The Incredible Power of Kingdom Authority*, p. 203. Nashville, TN: Broadman & Holman Publishers.

Week 11

1. Spurgeon, C. (2018) *The Golden Alphabet (Updated, Annotated): An Expostion of Psalm 119*. Abbotsford, WI: Aneko Press.

2. MacArthur, J. F., Jr. (2005). *2 Peter and Jude*, p. 123. Chicago, IL: Moody Publishers.

3. MacArthur, J. F., Jr. (2005). *2 Peter and Jude*, p. 128. Chicago, IL: Moody Publishers.

4. Henry, M. (1994). *Matthew Henry's Commentary on the Whole Bible: Complete and Unabridged in One Volume*, p. 2441. Peabody, MA: Hendrickson.

5. MacArthur, J. F., Jr. (2005). *2 Peter and Jude*, p. 135. Chicago, IL: Moody Publishers.

6. MacArthur, J. F., Jr. (2005). *2 Peter and Jude*, p. 135. Chicago, IL: Moody Publishers.

7. MacArthur, J. F., Jr. (1998). *James*, p. 49. Chicago, IL: Moody Press.

8. Rogers, A. (2017). Flawed Appetites and Fatal Attractions. In *Adrian Rogers Sermon Archive* (Jas 1:12–15). Signal Hill, CA: Rogers Family Trust.

9. MacArthur, J. F., Jr. (1998). *James*, p. 50. Chicago, IL: Moody Press.

10. Rogers, A. (2017). Flawed Appetites and Fatal Attractions. In *Adrian Rogers Sermon Archive* (Jas 1:12–15). Signal Hill, CA: Rogers Family Trust.

11. Giglio, L. (2017). *Goliath Must Fall: Winning the Battle Against Your Giants*, p. 54. Nashville, TN: Thomas Nelson.

12. Henry, M. (1994). *Matthew Henry's Commentary on the Whole Bible: Complete and Unabridged in One Volume*, p. 412. Peabody, MA: Hendrickson.

13. Logan, J. (1995). *Reclaiming Surrendered Ground: Protecting Your Family from Spiritual Attacks*, p. 33. Chicago, IL: Moody Publishers

14. Henry, M. (1994). *Matthew Henry's Commentary on the Whole Bible: Complete and Unabridged in One Volume*, pp. 412–413. Peabody, MA: Hendrickson.

15. Rogers, A. (2017). How to Hang Tough When the Going Gets Rough. In *Adrian Rogers Sermon Archive* (1 Pe 5:5–11). Signal Hill, CA: Rogers Family Trust.

16. Rogers, A. (2017). Real Salvation. In *Adrian Rogers Sermon Archive* (1 Jn 3:4–9). Signal Hill, CA: Rogers Family Trust.

Made in the USA
Lexington, KY
15 December 2018